How to Get Started in the
Real Estate Appraisal Business

How to Get Started in the

Real Estate Appraisal Business

Strategies to earn a six-figure salary

Daniel J. Nahorney

Foreword by Vicki Lankarge

McGraw-Hill

New York   Chicago   San Francisco   Lisbon   London
Madrid   Mexico City   Milan   New Delhi   San Juan
Seoul   Singapore   Sydney   Toronto

1 2 3 4 5 6 7 8 9 0   DOC/DOC   0 9 8 7 6

ISBN 0-07-146323-2

This publication is designed to provide accurate and authoritative information in regard to the subject matter covered. It is sold with the understanding that the publisher is not engaged in rendering legal, accounting, or other professional service. If legal advice or other expert assistance is required, the services of a competent professional person should be sought.
—From a declaration of principles jointly adopted by a committee
of the American Bar Association and a committee of publishers.

McGraw-Hill books are available at special quantity discounts to use as premiums and sales promotions, or for use in corporate training programs. For more information, please write to the Director of Special Sales, Professional Publishing, McGraw-Hill, Two Penn Plaza, New York, NY 10121-2298. Or contact your local bookstore.

 This book is printed on recycled, acid-free paper containing a minimum of 50% recycled, de-inked fiber.

Library of Congress Cataloging-in-Publication Data

Nahorney, Daniel J.
    How to get started in the real estate appraisal business / Dan Nahorney.
        p.   cm.
    Includes index.
    ISBN 0-07-146323-2 (alk. paper)
    1. Real property—Valuation—United States. 2. Real estate appraisers—Vocational guidance—United States. 3. Real estate appraisers—Certification—United States.
    4. New business enterprises—United States—Planning. I. Title.
    HD1389.5.U6N34 2006
    333.33'20681—dc22   2005037513

Contents

Contents

Foreword

know the author of this book pretty well. That's because Daniel J. Nahorney is my twin. Well, *technically* we have different mothers and were born in different years, but we're twins nonetheless.

This revelation dawned on me slowly. In 2000, we were writing and editing for a small dot com in West Hartford, Connecticut, when suddenly the tech sector went bust. Overnight, the company was smaller by a third. During its prolonged death throes, there was a kind of siege mentality. Dan and I hunkered down, brainstorming ways to preserve the Web site's reputation as one of the most respected consumer insurance information resources on the Internet. It was a blast.

Although the venture capital disappeared along with the promise of an IPO, we soldiered on. Our articles appeared on AOL, MSNBC, and CBS Marketwatch. The Columbia School of Journalism selected the Web site as a finalist in their first annual Online Journalism Awards for "General Excellence in Content Original to the Web." We lost the contest to Salon.com, but so did the Central Europe Review, CNET News, and TheStreet.com. It was heady stuff.

This is also when I discovered that Dan and I are actually twins who were separated in childhood and lived in some freakishly parallel universe. Both of us are veterans of small town newspapers where we each penned the classic "Sure Is Hot!" story every July and the "Sure Is Cold!" story every February.

Both of us are competitive. All it takes is for Dan to taunt me with, "Lankarge, you'll never get *that* information," and I'm off. Within seconds, I have a phone glued to my ear and my browser opened to Google. Likewise, if you tell Dan something is impossible—like buying his dream vacation home—stand back! If you look up the word *relentless* in the dictionary, there's a picture of Dan under the entry.

And both of us love to "talk shop," especially when it comes to real estate and home renovations. Long before I wrote *What Every Homeowner Needs to Know About Mold* (McGraw-Hill, 2003) and Dan and I partnered on *How to Increase the Value of Your Home* (McGraw-Hill, 2004), we routinely swapped war stories about the home improvements that made us proud, the ones that were utter train wrecks, and the others that just plain drove us crazy. In fact, Dan is so enthusiastic about his improvements that he has left one closet untouched from the days of his home's previous owners—just so he can show visitors the truly hideous original décor. He takes great delight in flinging open the closet door in his living room to reveal chartreuse and white stripes that narrow to a point on the ceiling like a miniature circus tent.

Dan's sense of fun is exceeded only by his depth of knowledge about the real estate market and home values. In *How to Get Started in the Real Estate Appraisal Business*, his ability to network with folks from the industry infuses his writing with life and wit. This "blood and bones" approach is what sets this book apart from the rest. There are plenty of "How to Become a Real Estate Appraiser" books on the market that are completely devoid of the human touch. This is not one of them.

The real estate appraisal profession is not a cinch to break into, but there is room for those who are willing to work hard to excel. Dan says leading real estate appraisers are like other professionals at the top of their games. "They are smart. They work hard. They demand excellence of themselves."

I will put aside any sibling rivalry and say Dan oughta know. He's describing himself.

Vicki Lankarge
West Hartford, Connecticut

Acknowledgments

Without the generosity of so many individuals this book would not have been possible. First I would like to thank my editors, Mary Glenn and Melissa Scuereb, for their guidance and assistance in shaping this book.

I would also like to thank the many outstanding real estate appraisers and professionals who support the profession and gave so generously of their time and expertise. Don Kelly and John Ross of the Appraisal Institute helped to provide much of the background for this book, as did Eric Goodman of the Lum Library. John Brenan and Paula Douglas of The Appraisal Foundation provided their expertise as well.

Appraisers who provided their expertise and firsthand experience included Julie Burkart, George Dell, Jeff Grendysa, Anne Johnson, Bruce Kellogg, Jack Miller, Dave Munsell, Frank O'Neill, Mark Pomykacz, Richard "Dick" Powers, and Doug Smith. I'd also like to thank Bob Johnson of the National Association of Real Estate Appraisers. Other appraisers who provided their expertise include John Aust, Al Franke, and Ann O'Rourke.

Acknowledgments

During the process of writing this book I learned that the real estate appraisal industry is truly in good hands—those of the leaders just mentioned.

I'd also like to thank Vicki Lankarge for her constant support during this process. Ned Mann, who helped to shape my career, provided hours of his insightful editing expertise for which I am grateful.

Finally, I'd like to thank my wife, Janet, for tolerating me during this process, and my children, Elizabeth, Kristen, and Stephen, for giving me the time to make this book a reality.

DANIEL J. NAHORNEY
djninc.com

Introduction

If you are intrigued by the real estate appraisal profession, this book is for you. Perhaps you are a real estate broker tired of the ups and downs of a career of sales. Perhaps you have grown weary of corporate America and wish to remove the ball and chain, get out of the office, and enjoy some fresh air during the day. Or maybe you are, or soon will be, a college graduate, and are looking to begin your career in a field that interests you.

Real estate appraisers are professionals who specialize in developing an opinion about the value of a piece of real estate. They are most commonly engaged during the sale or refinance of a piece of property, either residential or commercial.

Real estate appraisers are not home inspectors, who are typically hired by individuals or companies seeking to learn detailed information about the physical structure of a property. Appraisers are licensed professionals who do things such as research public records, review zoning maps, and get sales information about similar properties to help determine value. Appraisers frequently visit properties to make a physical review, doing things such as making a drawing of the building, examining any improvements that may have been made to it, and learning more about the surrounding properties.

In real estate sales, the appraiser is often the only neutral professional involved in the sales process. Both the selling and listing real estate agents' commissions are contingent on the new owners being able to get financing. The bank or mortgage company will only get paid if the appraiser's report shows that the value of the property is not less than the amount of the loan being requested. The buyer and seller have already negotiated a price they feel is fair. Appraisers can receive pressure from everyone involved in the sales process to "hit the number."

Looking for a quick answer about whether you should consider a real estate appraisal career? There is solid opportunity for those who enter the profession with the proper skills, start with a person or company dedicated to excellence, and push themselves to continue their education and take on increasingly more challenging work.

You'll enter the business as a *technician*. Those with the highest incomes become valued *analysts* and are paid much more than the average appraiser. Use this book as your personal roadmap to becoming an analyst.

The best real estate appraisers are not unlike other professionals at the top of their games. They are smart. They work hard. They demand excellence of themselves. They are community leaders. They are willing to put in the time and hard work necessary to become outstanding. They are always looking to grow as professionals. They give back to their profession by being active in their industry. They haven't become successful by accident, although they may have come into the industry by accident. They have become analysts and serve as valued consultants to their clients. They are very well paid.

Historically, the real estate appraising profession has been one that attracted those looking for a second career. Perhaps your friend or relative told you a little bit about the career and it seemed to appeal to you. Or you heard that an appraiser was looking for someone to help with the increasing workload. Or you are simply out of work, need to pay the bills, see a local appraiser driving a nice car, and would like one for yourself.

The appraisal profession was once a business people didn't choose, but rather fell into. But that is slowly changing as more recent college graduates are entering the career and technology has dramatically changed the way in which appraisers do their work. At the same time, many others looking for flexible hours, such as parents with small children and retirees, continue to be attracted to the profession because of its flexibility.

Through these pages you'll read about trends in the business and learn from industry experts about where they believe the industry is heading. And you'll learn that the profession is very different in rural areas from what it is in urban areas.

Not unlike most other professions today, nobody has a crystal ball that will show you exactly how the appraisal profession will change over the next 5 to 10 years. Yet we know a few things. The profession is "graying," so there is opportunity for those who enter the profession and learn quickly. However, the barriers to entry are high. Not only do you have to pass state mandated courses (the easy part), but you also need to find a mentor who will teach you the day-to-day parts of the job and will supervise you for 2,000 hours to become licensed (the hard part), and then pass a state licensing test.

Finding that mentor can be challenging. Residential appraising is a profession marked by long, deep cycles. During boom times it can seem like there are not enough appraisers to go around and, because most appraisers are paid based on the number of appraisals they complete, there can be a tendency for appraisers to overwork themselves—the "just one more" syndrome. Burnout can quickly occur.

Commercial appraising is marked by shorter cycles than residential appraising, and the difference between the top and the bottom can be much less dramatic in most areas.

There are about twice as many residential appraisers as commercial appraisers today, which seems pretty logical given how many more residential units there are than commercial buildings. But later in this book you'll learn that residential appraisers are much more likely than commercial appraisers to say there is too much competition.

Like many other businesses, the bulk of work is concentrated in the profession's lower-paying job assignments. However, the higher-paying assignments, where there is less competition, are fewer. Developing the skills that will qualify you for these higher-paying assignments takes time. But in the long run, as you'll hear over and over in these pages, the faster you become an analyst, the faster your pay will jump.

Industry experts say that to do the job one needs good mathematical and analytical skills, interpersonal skills, and writing skills. But perhaps the most important skill you will need to succeed is your ability to network successfully. That's because to get started you'll likely have to identify those appraisers who have the highest skills and highest integrity. These are the analysts for whom you'll want to work. You'll need networking skills to become well known in your community and profession. And like any business owner, you'll need strong networking skills to gain more business, whether for yourself or the company for which you'll work. You probably won't find a mentor looking in the help-wanted ads in the news-paper or online. You'll likely have to create your own opening. You'll need to use your networking skills to learn who the quality appraisers in your area are, and then you'll need to develop a plan for how to approach them.

Even after your initial training is complete, your education will have just begun. You'll need continuing education credits to keep your license. You'll also want to keep up-to-date on the latest industry trends. And you may want to consider an advanced designation to keep your career moving ahead.

When I first began interviewing appraisers for this book, the profession seemed very different from most others. As I said earlier, the barriers to entry are high. Pay is low to start. Much of the work comes in cycles. Most of those in the business operate out of their homes as sole proprietors. But then I saw the similarities to other professions—the fact that the industry has been radically changed by technology and that those who do as little as possible are forced to find different professions when times get tough.

Real estate appraisers perform invaluable services. During residential transactions, they can be the only professionals who are completely inde-pendent. For commercial transactions, they provide consultative services that buyers need to make critical business decisions.

Real estate appraising is a profession that offers both tangible and intangible rewards to those who challenge themselves to rise to the top of the profession. And as property values continue to escalate, it is a profession that will only grow in importance.

So here is the bottom line. For starters, you will not be paid anywhere near what some professionals who serve the real estate industry, such as lawyers and accountants, are paid. You'll be paid more like a beginning real estate broker, relatively little at first while you build your reputation.

But as many of the experts interviewed for this book will tell you, the profession is never boring, the work is challenging, every job is different, and being your own boss can be exhilarating. And for those who continue to grow as appraisers and become analysts, you'll never be forced to retire if you don't choose to retire; you can simply choose not to.

Now, if you're still thinking of exploring the real estate appraising profession, turn the page and let's get started!

How to Get
Started in the
Real Estate
Appraisal
Business

PART ONE

Looking in at the profession

1

A five-step process

Becoming a licensed real estate appraiser is a five-step process.

1. Investigate the career
2. Pass state-mandated appraisal courses
3. Find a licensed appraiser to supervise you for 2,000 hours
4. Work those 2,000 hours
5. Pass the state real estate appraisal license test

As with any new career you are considering, you should spend considerable time investigating whether the real estate appraisal career is for you. One of the best ways to do this is to activate your network. Talk with your relatives, friends, and neighbors about anyone they know who may be a real estate appraiser. Also, talk with real estate agents, accountants, and bankers who also may know appraisers.

Work to get contacts with as many appraisers as possible, and then contact them to schedule informational interviews with them. During an informational interview, you are not interviewing for a job, but rather trying to get a feel for exactly what the real estate appraisal job entails, determining whether you have the skills necessary to excel, and whether the job interests you. Some of the questions you may want to ask include the following:

- Why did you enter the real estate appraisal business?
- What do the successful real estate appraisers you know have in common?
- What skills do you look for in new trainees?
- Why do some trainees succeed and others fail?
- What do you do in the course of an average day?
- What parts of your job most interest you?
- What parts of the job don't you like to do?
- What is the most difficult part of your job?
- How do you see the real estate appraisal profession changing in the next few years? How will that change affect how you do business?
- What types of appraisals do you specialize in? Why?
- How strong is the local real estate appraisal market?
- How many hours do you work in an average week? Are those hours flexible?
- Are there too few, enough, or too many appraisers serving the local market?
- Is the market for local appraisers increasing, decreasing, or staying the same?
- How has technology changed the way you do business?
- Do you hire people with no appraisal experience? If so, please describe your training program.

Additionally, because breaking into the profession requires that you have a licensed appraiser supervise you for 2,000 hours, you should inquire whether the appraiser might consider hiring you in the future, and whether his or her appraisal company could support another appraiser in the near future. And, of course, before you leave you should ask for referrals to other appraisers so that you can conduct additional informational interviews to get a well-rounded view of the profession.

State courses and tests

Next, you will likely need to pass state-mandated courses (some states also have provisional or intern licenses). While this isn't a national requirement, most appraisers will not seriously consider you as a potential trainee unless you have shown the initiative to spend the time and money to take and pass these courses.

Currently, states require about 75 hours of training, most often composed of three courses (see Appendix 4 for an outline of the topics covered in these courses):

- Basic Appraisal Principles
- Basic Appraisal Procedures
- Uniform Standards of Professional Appraisal Practice (USPAP) overview

In most states, especially in the more populated areas, you will likely have your choice of taking courses from either trade associations or for-profit companies. To find the exact requirements in your state, see Appendix 8.

To determine which organizations will best prepare you for a real estate appraisal career, be sure to ask the appraisers during your informational interviews. Some organizations will sport glossy course brochures or slick Web sites, but asking those who have taken the courses about their quality can help you select the best choice and get your career off to a strong start.

Remember, when taking these courses you want to gain valuable knowledge that you will draw upon for your entire career. Courses that focus on passing the test, rather than learning basic real estate appraisal information, are less valuable to you in the long run.

Passing the state licensing test is a challenge—especially for those who aren't adequately prepared. The test is not a pushover, and you will need to put in the time to ensure that you are prepared for it by spending time studying over several months

After passing the state licensing test, keys to a successful career include continually challenging yourself to learn new skills to better serve your local market. Many successful appraisers take continuing education courses calculated to increase their knowledge of their profession, oftentimes learning key information about new types of appraisals they wish to specialize in.

Finding a supervisor

Finding someone to supervise you for the 2,000 on-the-job hours (usually over two years) required by most states is often the most challenging part of entering the business (see Chapter 4). That is why it is important for you to get a good feel for the strength of the local appraisal market during your informational interviews. You will need to spend the time up front to make sure that the market will be sufficiently strong to provide you with a job once you pass the introductory courses.

Working those 2,000 hours can be tough. As with any new profession, you will at first find it challenging to feel like you are making a strong contribution to the success of the appraiser who has hired you. But if you have chosen the right supervisor/mentor, you will quickly begin gaining the skills you will need to build a successful career.

Appraisal is a tough profession to enter, but reading the success stories presented throughout this book can help you to chart your course to the top of the profession.

2

So, you want to become an appraiser

This chapter describes why:

- Math and analytical skills are important, but writing skills are, too.
- Industry changes have come quickly due to technology.
- Urban and rural appraisers operate very differently.

There are about 71,000 licensed real estate appraisers in the United States. These appraisers receive in total about $5.1 billion in fees per year.

The 2004 Appraisal Institute Member Survey shows that appraisers earned an average of $85,500 from real estate appraisal services. Average incomes differed by type of appraiser:

- Principal/partners of appraisal firms reported average incomes of $120,000.

- Sole proprietors reported average incomes of about $85,000.
- Employee/contractors reported average incomes of about $72,000.

Furthermore:

- 16 percent reported incomes of $150,000 or more.
- 9 percent of the previous group reported earning $200,000 or more.
- 8 percent reported incomes below $40,000.

Getting in

Some businesses are easy to get into. The pay for rookies is good. The hours are regular. The work is consistent. The training is standardized—all you need to do is follow the track laid out for you, work hard, and you'll reach the pot of gold at the end of the rainbow.

When it comes to real estate appraising, the opposite is closer to the truth. You would be hard pressed to find a single appraiser who would tell you it is easy to enter the business; that you don't have to work very hard to make a great living; and that you'll be making a lot of money within two years.

Successful real estate appraisers are a tough breed. Most have paved their own roads to success. Most will tell you it is very difficult to break into the business; it is challenging to move from being a trainee to being an appraiser; and developing steady work takes a long time. And even when you have "made it," external events such as a jump in interest rates, a recession, a real estate bubble that bursts, or a generally weak economy can damage your ability to earn a good living.

Find an appraiser who has all the work he or she needs and chances are that he or she:

- Has worked very hard to succeed
- Has carved out a niche
- And/or is working in a vibrant economy

Those who work hard to succeed earn six-figure incomes, enjoy flexible hours that allow them to spend quality time with their families, and are looked upon as leaders in their profession. Many of the top appraisers

Take the appraisal quiz

Ready for a quick exercise to tell you whether you could excel in the real estate appraisal business?

Answer each of the following questions by circling either 1, 2, or 3 where 1=disagree; 2=neither agree nor disagree, and 3=agree.

1. I would like a job in which I am able to determine my ability to get ahead by how hard I work. 1 2 3
2. I'm the type of person who needs a supervisor to get me started, but then I want the freedom to complete the job on my own. 1 2 3
3. I am comfortable using technology to better complete tasks and I frequently look for better ways to get the job done. 1 2 3
4. I have the ability to independently analyze information and form logical conclusions. 1 2 3
5. Crunching numbers is something I enjoy. 1 2 3
6. I have the ability to take complex information and write a detailed report about that information that others can easily understand. 1 2 3
7. I view constructive criticism as a growing experience. 1 2 3
8. I like the challenge of being confronted with different jobs every day. 1 2 3
9. Becoming a dinosaur frightens me—I'm looking for a profession where continuing education is required. 1 2 3
10. I understand that starting a new profession will be challenging: I'll likely begin doing menial tasks, the pay will likely not be high to start, and the hours may be long. 1 2 3

Tally your total score.

If you scored less than 15 points, this might not be the profession for you, or you will at least need to dramatically change your

(*Continued*)

expectations. Read this book carefully to determine whether you should proceed.

If you scored 16 to 22 points, you have some of the skills and attributes you will need. Read on to learn what others have done to get off to a strong start and what they have done to build a successful career.

If you scored 23 or more points, read quickly so you can find out what you need to get your career off and running!

profiled throughout this book spend no time seeking additional clients—they have built strong businesses based on their reputation for quality and provide the highest level of service to their clients.

Others, who often work as independent contractors who aren't aiming for the top of the appraisal profession, look to the industry for an average income with above-average flexibility.

What do successful appraisers have in common?

Many people enter the appraisal business as a second career, often with diverse backgrounds. Based on interviews with top appraisers, more appraisers entering the business today have four-year college degrees, often in business, mathematics, or English. Frank O'Neill, a 20-year appraisal veteran who has taught appraisal techniques for 12 years, says that most successful appraisers have an analytical streak. They have to be able to write reports that people can understand, and the reports must be convincing.

Going forward, appraisers who don't embrace technology will likely have a difficult time succeeding. Those who are early adopters of technology may see their earning power increase.

Appraisers need a good aptitude with math because they will be doing analyses, measuring rooms and totaling square footage, and reviewing other sales information to make a determination on a property's value.

Appraisers also need to be part detective as they investigate a property to determine its value.

Appraisers need to be self-starters. The speed at which you progress in the career will be determined in large part by the initiative you take to learn the job, ask for more detailed work, and learn enough to begin measuring properties on your own. Self-starters will find new markets, new ways to accomplish tasks more quickly, and new clients to keep their businesses growing.

Appraisers need thick skin, especially when starting out. The job will likely be all new to you. That means mistakes, and your supervisor will be correcting your work. It can be very frustrating if you aren't able to accept constructive criticism.

What may come as a surprise to you is that appraisers need strong writing skills. Candidates will quickly learn that after the physical work of taking measurements comes the analytical work—followed by the narrative report. The best investigators can gather all of the information needed to make a valuation determination, but if the information isn't conveyed in a logical, easy-to-understand manner in the narrative report, then the person reading the report may not understand how the conclusions were drawn. That can result in not getting additional work from that company.

Where has the industry been?

The real estate appraising industry has been one that has attracted a large number of its ranks from those looking for a second career. Industry experts say this is at least partly true because the profession is not one that has undergraduate degrees in colleges across the country as do other business professions such as accounting. There also isn't the sort of structure that would provide young candidates with a clear-cut career path, nor do new appraisers have the ability to earn a whole lot in the first year. Because of this, few college graduates in the past were attracted to the profession.

How appraisals get done was also dramatically different in the past. Buildings were always inspected in person, both externally and internally, and getting appointments to get access to the buildings could take time. Buildings were measured by hand with measuring tapes; pictures were taken using cameras with film, which then needed to be processed (taking about a week); sketches were done by hand; and forms were filled out by hand. Then the reports were typed up (with the help of a lot of correcting tape), photos were attached to the report, and all was mailed back to the requester.

A challenging part of the business was finding "comparables," or properties that were similar in size and location so that an accurate determination could be made about the value of the property just inspected. In the past, comparables in urban areas would be obtained by talking with real estate brokers, people who recently sold their homes, town assessors, and perhaps town or county clerks who recorded sales. The smaller the community, the more of a challenge it was for appraisers to find quality comparables.

The whole process for completing a residential appraisal would easily take a week: from receiving the order to receiving an appointment to visit the property, to examining and measuring the property, to typing up the report, to waiting for the pictures to be returned, and, finally, to mailing the report. Getting things done in a day or two was virtually impossible but, then again, bank loans would take about a month to be approved, so rapid turnaround was not critical.

Like most businesses before overnight couriers, fax machines, and e-mail, things moved slower. Processes simply weren't in place for a turnaround that would be considered "fast" by today's standards.

Things began to change in the late 1970s as momentum began to increase for licensing. The idea that began the licensing movement was that licensing would increase the level of professionalism across the country.

Then in the late 1980s, when the savings and loan crisis hit, licensing became reality. By the mid 1990s, real estate appraisal licensing was a requirement in every state.

Where is the industry today?

"The industry has evolved to the point where we want it faster, we want it cheaper, and we probably want it better," says Jeff Grendysa, SRA, a mortgage banker for a bank in southeast Michigan. "In the past, if you closed a mortgage in a month you were a superstar. Today you can close a loan in two weeks, and in some instances quicker, depending on the type of the loan," says Grendysa.

Like every industry, technology has dramatically changed how real estate appraisers get their work, do their work, and submit their work. Appraisers with an established clientele now conduct much of their business using e-mail.

Not every appraisal requires a physical inspection today. The credit score of the person or persons requesting the loan, along with the loan-to-value ratio, can determine the extent of the appraisal requested. *Automated Valuation Models* (AVMs) have taken on some of the loan work that does not require a physical inspection. AVMs—computer software that helps perform appraisals—have had a dramatic effect on those residential real estate appraisers who specialize in basic appraisal reports in well-populated areas.

Instead of using tape measures, many appraisers today use laser tools to more quickly and accurately measure structures, easily shaving the time spent on site by half. Some appraisers use software to sketch the property.

The narrative portion of the average appraisal report is longer, but that isn't a problem because of computer software. Gone are typewriters, along with the endless corrections, replaced with software programs that allow appraisers to quickly populate fields to provide quality reports.

Obtaining data with which to review comparables has gotten much easier in the more urban areas, with the use of databases of sales information. Appraisers oftentimes have at their fingertips volumes of information—the key remains selecting those properties that are comparable to the property that is being appraised.

Although the average cost of a typical real estate appraisal has changed little over the past 20 years, appraisers are nonetheless earning more money on average than they did 20 years ago, thanks to technology. Those who have embraced technology have seen their incomes rise rapidly.

Although the cost of appraisals is almost always a flat fee, appraisers determine that fee based on the hours it will take to complete the appraisal. Technology has enabled appraisers to cut the amount of time it takes to complete an assignment in several ways:

- Assignments come into the office via e-mail, often in a similar format, saving processing time.
- Many appraisals today don't require a physical interior inspection.
- Appraisers who use electronic tools to measure those jobs that do require a physical inspection can often cut their time on site in half.
- Accompanying photos are now digital, eliminating the time and cost of using film. Appraisers can simply download digital photos into their computers and then electronically insert them into the final appraisal reports.
- Electronic forms allow the appraiser to quickly fill in the necessary data.
- Completed forms in .pdf form can be e-mailed back to clients.

So those early adopters of technology today have a well-oiled system in place that allows them to easily complete in a day a detailed appraisal report that formerly took them a week. And a report that formerly took days to complete can often now be turned around in the same day.

Where is the industry heading?

As with virtually every other profession, technology will have a continuing and dramatic impact on how appraisals get done. Today, appraisers in urban areas have databases of sales information at their fingertips that can be used to find comparables. Typically, appraisers in rural areas still need strong networking skills in order to gain information they need to find comparables. These networking skills are useful for obtaining sales information from real estate agents, mortgage officers, and town clerks who record deeds. Because of this, there can be less competition in rural areas than in urban areas.

Some of those appraisers who were in favor of making licensing a reality are dismayed because they believe it hasn't improved the industry's overall professionalism. These people believe that licensing has put all real estate appraisers on nearly the same footing and feel that this is far from the truth. Many who led the original fight for licensing are now rethinking their stand.

AVMs (Automated Valuation Models) have been around for about 20 years, and they are here to stay. They will likely continue to take market share away from those residential appraisers who focus on the most basic types of appraisals. What may occur is that AVMs may enter into the commercial side of the real estate profession, providing another tool for commercial appraisers to use and for loan officers to consider when making or evaluating loans. AVMs will be discussed at greater length in Chapter 11.

Commercial appraisers will likely have more databases of sales information at their fingertips to help them determine a property's value. And an increasing number of residential appraisers located outside of urban areas will likely have access to more databases of sales information, lessening the time needed to complete appraisals.

Work to smooth out the cycles– a conversation with Richard Powers

The biggest long-term challenge of the real estate appraisal profession is overcoming the long, deep market cycles. But becoming a student of the industry can provide you with the information necessary to develop specialties that may be countercyclical to each other, therefore providing you with the ability to continue to make a good living, despite the economic conditions.

Richard "Dick" Powers, MAI, SRA, 2006 president of the Appraisal Institute, says the key to the appraisal profession is getting involved with professional associations from day one. Powers says that even before entering the business, involvement in a professional association as an associate member will provide you with firsthand information, not only about the profession, but also about the best appraisers. Armed with this knowledge, you are better able to target high-quality appraisers as potential mentor candidates and learn from industry leaders early in your career. "And you can form relationships that can level out those cycles a little better," says Powers. Relationships with top appraisers can provide you with valuable insight into the various subsets of the profession, helping you identify different areas in which you might want to specialize and build a business for the long term. Your specialties can all be in residential or commercial, or a combination of the two. The key is finding those specialties in your region that are large enough to support you and that don't all react to economic conditions in the same manner.

Powers says that to get an accurate picture of your region's marketplace, your network should include not only top appraisers, but also realtors, lenders, attorneys, and accountants.

Getting his start

Powers, owner and president of Powers, Smith & Associates in Keene, New Hampshire, a city of about 23,000 residents, began his career as a mortgage loan officer in a local bank. The person in charge of the loan department made loan decisions and was also the appraiser. As the job expanded, this person didn't have time to complete all of the appraisals himself, so he posted the job.

Becoming a real estate appraiser in a bank seemed like a good challenge, so Powers applied and got the job. After seven years, he decided to strike out on his own. He began with a one-room office. Technology at the time consisted of an electric typewriter. Not being a good typist, he hired a secretary to type the appraisal reports.

He steadily grew his business, eventually adding a partner a couple of years ago in order to free up time for his Appraisal Institute duties (he is on the road 100 to 120 days per year). He has three commercial and four residential appraisers on staff—during the 1980s boom he had as many as 12 people working for him.

Over the years, Powers has developed appraisal specialties, including gas stations, convenience stores, hotels, and golf courses. "In rural areas you end up doing a little of everything," explains Powers, adding that in large metropolitan areas you can develop much narrower specialties. Overall, Powers concentrates his energies in residential appraisals in Cheshire County, New Hampshire, and commercial work that is no more than an hour away from his Keene office.

Entering the business

Powers says that trainees entering the business today are often younger, have stronger technical skills, and possess more analytic ability than those 20 or 30 years ago. He says that trainees today need to analyze the profession and decide which area they want to specialize in—the goal being to move from being a technician to becoming a valued analyst.

For those looking for quality mentors, Powers urges people not only to join local chapters of appraisal associations, but also to talk with local lenders and attorneys to learn whose appraisal report work they most value.

Powers offers this advice: As your career progresses, be sure your goals with continuing education are to stretch your mind to learn about new techniques, and perhaps to open your eyes to new markets that may be underserved. "Twenty hours a year [of continuing education] might not be enough to keep up with the changes coming over the next five years," says Powers. "The profession will likely change at a quickening pace," he says, and he predicts that the pace of change might double or triple over the next five years.

The future is bright for residential and commercial appraisers—both for those seeking positions as independent contractors and for those aiming for the top of the profession.

PART TWO

From outsider to trainee

3

Courses you'll need to get started

This chapter describes why:

- To be licensed, you need about 2,000 hours of supervised experience and to pass a state test.

- Choosing top-quality classes yields long-term results.

- State licensing tests are challenging.

Because of the savings and loan crisis of the 1980s, when many savings and loans went bankrupt because of bad loans, Congress enacted a law that states that the federally regulated financial institutions—such as federally insured banks, thrifts, and credit unions—must use state-certified or licensed appraisers to perform appraisals. In 1994 additional federal guidelines limited this requirement to residential transactions of more than $250,000.

Licenses are granted by each state, and requirements differ. In general, you will need to pass several courses to be considered for employment by an appraiser. Some states have a provisional license that trainees receive after passing several courses. Next, you will need about 2,000 hours of experience supervised by a state-licensed appraiser. Finally, to become a fully licensed appraiser, you will need a passing grade on the state licensing exam.

The difficult part of this process is that you will be taking the courses that help you to prepare for the state test about two years prior to the exam. That means that students who put in the work to really learn the material (not just enough work to pass the test at the end of the course) will likely fare better when it comes to taking the state licensing test.

For example, students who complete the required reading assignments prior to class and then come in with questions to discuss in class to further their understanding of the subjects will likely fare better when taking a licensing test. Additionally, students who study for the state tests over an extended period of time, rather than trying to cram the week prior to the test, will likely have better results. As with most situations, you'll get out of the classes what you put into them in time and energy.

Frank O'Neill, SRA, a partner in O'Neill, Duffy & Co., in Danbury, Connecticut, recommends that his students purchase and study the book *The Appraisal of Real Estate,* published by the Appraisal Institute to help them prepare for the state licensing test. O'Neill calls this book the most authoritative appraisal textbook available. O'Neill has also developed a review course for candidates seeking to become state licensed, culling subject matter from the more than 12 years of classroom training he has delivered. Other courses are available that also provide students with a good overview of subjects that will likely be covered on the licensing tests.

Specific appraisal licensing requirements are set on a state-by-state basis, so to learn the requirements for your state, contact your state department that handles appraisal licenses. This could be a separate appraisal department, a business and professional services department, or a department of professional licensure. (See Appendix 8 for state-by-state contact information.)

Common requirements

For example, here are the requirements for the State of New York. These requirements are common to other states as well.

Category	Requirement
Licensed appraiser	90 hours of education
State-certified residential appraiser	120 hours of education
State-certified general appraiser	180 hours of education

Further, New York requirements include the following:

- To become a licensed appraiser: 2,000 hours of experience over a period of not less than two years, 1,500 hours of which must be in the form of appraisals of residential properties listed in a state *Appraisal Experience Report*.
- To become a state-certified residential appraiser: 2,500 hours of experience over a period of not less than 24 months, 1,875 hours of which must be in the form of properties listed in a state *Appraisal Experience Report*.
- To become a state-certified general appraiser: 3,000 hours of experience over a period of not less than two years, 2,250 hours of which must be in the form of appraisals of general properties listed in a state *Appraisal Experience Report*.

General experience must contain experience in multifamily, commercial/industrial, or other (land/manufacturing/institutional) appraisals. Sixty percent of the general experience must be in one of the above categories; 20 percent of the general experience must be in the remaining two categories.

Check with the state in which you plan to become licensed for the most up-to-date requirements.

Basic education

The required education in many states most often includes the following three courses:

- Basic Appraisal Principles
- Basic Appraisal Procedures
- Uniform Standards of Professional Appraisal Practice (USPAP) overview

Tests follow each of the classes. O'Neill says the pass rate for the Basic Appraisal Principles and Basic Appraisal Procedures courses is about 90 percent. The test following the USPAP course is much more difficult, with pass rates of about 70 to 80 percent.

Different formats for taking these classes are available (be sure to check with your state to see which are accepted). The most common format is the classroom. Often the courses are taught two nights per week for six weeks. For new trainees, it is possible, using this format, to complete the three classes in about four months.

Other classroom courses meet for 10 hours a day for three days in a row, while still others include online options.

Tough test

Individual state licensing tests are based on an outline developed by the Appraisal Qualifications Board (AQB). Most appraisers agree that the state licensure tests are challenging. Most applicants take the courses prior to becoming a trainee (many appraisers won't consider trainees who haven't passed the state-mandated courses). That means you'll likely begin taking classes while still employed or in school, but won't sit for the test until two years later.

Trainees who successfully pass the state licensing tests are usually enrolled in courses taught by quality instructors who focus on imparting knowledge rather than simply preparing trainees for tests. How do you find those quality instructors? When investigating the career, be sure to ask appraisers about which classes and instructors they recommend.

Some organizations also request student feedback about classes and instructors. These organizations sometimes look for alternate instructors when the student test pass rate declines, or when student feedback is negative.

Top appraiser instructors say that trainees need to keep their course books close by during their first 2,000 hours in order to keep the information fresh and to be sure they are using the knowledge gleaned during those courses while on the job.

The test for residential appraisers often includes questions covering the three approaches to value:

1. Sales comparison
2. Cost approach
3. Income approach

Trainees taking the test to become residential appraisers often assume they only need to know information about the sales comparison approach, perhaps the most common approach when valuing single-family homes. However, the outline provided by the AQB for developing state tests does include information about the basics of all three approaches.

Additionally, candidates seeking to pass the state licensing test to become general or commercial appraisers need to understand how a discounted cash flow analysis works (more on this later).

It's a family tradition–a conversation with Jack Miller

It seemed like the family thing to do. Thirty-four years ago, Jack Miller followed in his father's and grandfather's footsteps and entered the real estate appraisal profession. Miller's father, like many who have pursued the profession, became an appraiser in his late 20s when he was between jobs. At the time there was no licensing or formal training, but he got his start like others back then, jumping in as a trainee, pounding out reports on a typewriter.

Career crossroads

Miller worked to establish his own appraisal business, then came to a career crossroads. Faced with a decision either to grow the business or to accept a position with a national sub-prime lender, he decided on the latter. He liked the long-term possibilities the position held and the fact that he would be able to use all of the skills he had developed during his early years in the profession.

The job, as collateral risk manager for the CIT Group, also offered the advantage of being located just about anywhere the mail can be delivered and the Internet can be accessed. Miller relocated from California to Billingham, Washington, in early 2005 to get away from the expense and the crowds of California.

As a collateral risk manager, Miller reviews appraisal reports for one- to four-family houses that are completed by other appraisers, and he reviews the entire loan to determine how secure the lender's investment is. Because people who use sub-prime lenders have less-than-perfect credit, reviewing the collateral (the property) becomes even more important. In their review, Miller and his 12 peers across the country examine the appraisal, the type of loan requested, whether any cash is coming back out, and the credit history of the owners. Most of the time, two to three reviews can be completed per hour, although others can take an hour and a half or more.

"We are more interested in the bottom line," says Miller, adding that they review the photographs of the property more than anything else in the report.

Starting today

The profession is much different today from when Miller started out. He says he made more than $20,000 as an appraiser right out of high school in 1971. Today, new appraisers earn less, need to become licensed, and take continuing education to maintain that license.

With the profession graying, there has been an increase in the number of trainees entering the business in California, although nationwide the number of trainees has remained low.

The challenge for trainees is finding the right mentors, but Miller sees more experienced appraisers willing to work with people new to the profession. When experienced appraisers are busy, they are more likely to take on trainees since they are looking for ways to improve their efficiency by balancing their workloads.

Miller urges trainees to interview several potential mentors to make an informed decision. Some appraisers may not have strong business skills to impart to trainees, thus stunting trainees' growth.

Miller also urges trainees to find the most active local chapter of a local appraisal organization to benefit from interaction with quality appraisers.

4

It's time to find a quality mentor

This chapter describes why:

- You should first find high-quality appraisers.
- You should next develop a 30-second elevator speech about what you bring to the table.
- Finally, you should convince a quality appraiser that you are the best candidate to hire.

Want to know the secret that many top appraisers have used to get their careers off and running, quickly moving far ahead of other trainees who entered the business at the same time? Find the best mentor near where you live to go to work for, work as hard as you can for him or her, and then emulate the skills he or she has used to get to the top.

Learning from an appraiser who has worked his or her way to becoming an analyst will provide you the specific skills, work ethic, and overall knowledge you will need to succeed in this business.

Not much help to the bottom line

To become a licensed appraiser, you need a supervisor to sign your reports and to provide you with the approximately 2,000 hours of training. You'll likely receive a low salary during the first two years as this training is taking place. That is because, during your first year, your ability to add to the bottom line for the firm for which you are working will probably be limited. As someone new to the profession, you will be doing mostly menial work and will need supervision to complete reports. That means that, although you can assist your supervisor, at least at first you'll likely cause your supervisor to work longer hours to teach you the ropes.

A general rule in the industry is that a trainee costs the mentor money during the first year, but can make money for the mentor during the second year when the trainee is able to do more work unsupervised. Of course, all work must be reviewed for your first 2,000 hours on the job as you earn your license.

There is no "typical" mentor program. The largest group of appraisers are those who are sole proprietors, so you may be working out of someone's home, which has its own unique challenges. Although there are fewer appraisal firms than sole proprietor appraisers, anecdotal information suggests that the firms are far more likely to take on trainees because they already understand how to add staff and make money in doing so. Appraisal firms in a growth mode are always looking for candidates with specific skill sets, especially those who can help fill a void among their current staff.

For example, Doug Smith says his latest trainee is a wizard at Microsoft Word and Excel, has used various bookkeeping software programs, and has experience running an office. This trainee added significant value to his office, so he was willing to take her on. If you have unique skills like these and can find the appraiser who needs them, you could have a good match.

Because appraisers want to complete reports better, faster, and cheaper, and 30 percent of appraisers are over age 55, a younger person with strong computer and technology skills could be of great value to a mentor who needs these skills.

Why not?

Appraisers can be reluctant to bring on trainees for several reasons:

- Some are terrified of the liability. If a trainee completes part of a report incorrectly and the mentor doesn't catch it, that problem could eventually result in the appraiser losing his or her license.
- Many appraisers work out of their own homes (about 40 percent are sole proprietors), and they don't want strangers in the privacy of their homes.
- Some appraisers realize they don't know how to properly train someone new to the business, while others simply don't want the hassle that goes with mentoring a new person.
- It costs money. Pay for trainees is minimal, but that pay comes from money that would be paid to the others in the firm. At least at first, the trainee is unlikely to have a positive impact on the bottom line.

Now that you understand why appraisers might not want to bring on trainees, you'll need to overcome such objections by projecting an image that shows:

- You can be trusted.
- You are detail oriented.
- You are eager to learn.
- You would be easy to train.
- You are a fast study and are willing to put in the time necessary to quickly get up to speed.
- You will learn so quickly and do such high-quality work that you will quickly provide a return for any investment in you of time and money.

A quality mentor

How do you find a quality mentor? Well, certainly not in the newspaper or online employment sites. Finding a quality mentor can set the tone for your entire appraisal career, so it is imperative that you have a game plan to find one who will help you to succeed.

The best way to find a quality mentor is to network with other real estate appraisers (perhaps by attending their functions) and with other professionals serving the real estate profession, such as mortgage bankers and real estate brokers. Ask as many people as you can which appraisers have the best reputations for providing the highest quality work. You'll need to ask quite a few people because you'll likely receive a wide variety of responses.

Perhaps you'll receive the name of two or three top appraisers in your region—that's good. Then you'll need to convince one of them that you will be an asset to him or her.

Don't settle for just any trainee opening that you might find. Your goal is to find the best appraisers in the area in which you wish to specialize—residential or commercial—and then target them.

What will that quality appraiser look for in a trainee candidate? Someone who:

- Will work hard and is determined to succeed despite obstacles
- Shows initiative
- Knows a significant amount about the appraisal industry
- Can be an asset to the firm, perhaps with a skill set that is complementary to those already on board
- Is like the quality appraiser in that the trainee appears to be willing to give back to the profession

Get moving

If you aren't working on passing the state licensing exams yet, get moving. Then you have to do a lot of research into the real estate profession. For starters, use the appendixes of this book and dive into the resources listed to learn as much as you can.

You'll also learn quickly by joining a real estate appraisal professional organization, attending meetings, and reading appraisal magazines and Web sites. Becoming familiar with the field you are about to enter is critical. Your long-term goal is to become an expert in the niche in which you choose to specialize.

You should also complete a personal skill assessment to help identify what skills you can bring to a professional appraisal office. Perhaps your personal network includes mortgage bankers or real estate professionals, or perhaps your background includes work in the construction field and you can quickly assess the quality of a building, or maybe you keep up on the latest technology and can bring these skills to the office.

You must develop a well-rehearsed 30-second "elevator speech" that highlights your key skills and what you can bring to the appraisal office you are targeting. That's because the first time you meet your targeted mentor this may be all the time you have, and you'll certainly want to make a good impression.

Get to know your mentor

From there, you will want to get to know your potential mentor, seeking to ensure that your personalities are complementary and confirming that he or she is a person of integrity. Remember, while you are assessing possible mentors, they will be determining if you are the kind of person they want in their organizations.

Appraisal organizations can also help to pair you with a potential mentor. The Appraisal Institute, a national organization with chapters across the United States, offers a free service that can help you identify appraisers who are looking for trainees. Check their Web site at www.appraisalinstitute.org for more information.

Finding a quality mentor can be difficult. But for those who are dedicated to putting in the time necessary to find a quality mentor to learn and grow from, the process can be rewarding. And getting off on the right foot in this profession means that you are building your career on strong footing that will generate rewards for years to come.

Find a quality mentor–a conversation with Frank O'Neill

About 20 years ago in Connecticut, Frank O'Neill, SRA, went to work for his wife's uncle in the real estate appraisal business. O'Neill bought him out a year later, and today he manages a successful business, O'Neill, Duffy & Co., in Danbury, Connecticut.

O'Neill, who has also been teaching appraisers for 12 years, was a 10-year member of the Appraisal Institute board of directors and also served as a local chapter president. O'Neill's business has included up to 15 employees, and he currently has 3. In the Connecticut market, appraisers had been desperate for additional help in the past few years as business boomed, and more trainees have since entered the business.

O'Neill says that new appraisers today most often have four-year college degrees along with an analytical streak that helps them to succeed.

Finding a mentor

According to O'Neill, those looking to enter the business need to spend the time necessary to find a quality mentor—someone who will work closely with you and provide the strong background necessary to succeed. "The big challenge is finding a place to break in," says O'Neill.

Candidates who appear to be more attractive to potential mentors include those with real estate experience, often as real estate agents; those who may know something about the real estate market; those with advanced degrees; or those who embrace technology and who can help bring an office to the next level.

O'Neill has seen situations where one appraiser had 10 to 20 trainees at once, and he questions whether the trainees could have received an appropriate level of support and training. Training that may be limited to passing the basic appraisal courses, being handed a clipboard, and then being sent out into the field is not anywhere near adequate.

O'Neill says that trainees who start work for him are given lots of one-on-one time because he realizes that the more time he spends with them early, the quicker they will learn the ropes, and the better their chances of succeeding. He adds that trainees need a balance of experience and knowledge to go on to be successful appraisers.

Mentors hope that trainees stay long enough for the trainees to repay the time spent with them in the initial stages of training, when their pay did not match their productivity.

The next level

Appraisers who want to succeed long term should take continuing education courses that build upon their analyst skills. At the same time, they should be looking to see how well they fit in with the rest of their organization and how they can complement the skills of their peers.

To continue to grow their businesses, appraisers need to be students of their local market conditions so they can ramp up their marketing should they detect a softening market. Different parts of the real estate market react differently to changes in the economy. For example, condominium sales may be strong, while multifamily home sales might be weak.

In the beginning, appraisers will need to work to get themselves on lenders' approved appraiser lists. A good start in this direction is to contact lenders directly to learn how to become approved.

To make your income jump, you'll need to work harder or more efficiently, observes O'Neill, adding that newer appraisers who are on their own may wish to take on assignments from other appraisal offices or appraisal management firms, receiving a split fee instead of an entire fee. Appraisal companies commonly split the fee 50-50 with appraisers who are hired to complete reports.

"You need to find a way to start developing your own clients. Effective networking and good client relations are the base of a strong appraisal business."

Earning more

Although a typical part-time residential appraiser might earn $15,000 per year, full-time residential appraisers can earn $100,000 per year or more. It all depends on how efficient you are and what kind of work you do, says O'Neill. For example, many appraisers don't want to have anything to do with an appraisal when there is litigation or a threat of litigation, but for those who are confident of their skills and comfortable being on the witness stand, the pay is much higher than that earned on the typical residential appraisal.

5

A day in the life of an appraiser

This chapter describes why:

- You need to develop a thick skin—it will be tough at first.

- You must make a big decision once you pass the second-year mark.

- You must keep the goal of becoming a valued analyst in mind.

Beginning any new career can be overwhelming. You probably don't know the people you will be working with, so getting to know the personalities can take time. The work is all new, so it is difficult to be able to add a lot of value early on. The systems are all new as well. It is easy to get frustrated, feel inadequate, and be ready to walk out the door at a moment's notice. But, as Douglas Smith, IFAS, an appraiser in Montana says, "The job triangle is skills, knowledge, and attitude. Attitude is the most important."

Your attitude is the one thing that is entirely under your control. You can set your attitude when you wake up in the morning, choosing to be positive, upbeat, determined not to allow yourself to be brought down. Or you can set your attitude based on the attitudes of those around you or based on what happens to you during the day.

Getting your appraisal career off to a strong start is going to take a strong will and a great attitude. Yes, everything will be new. You might not be working for the best supervisor in the world, and he or she may expect too much of you at first. Or perhaps your supervisor won't challenge you enough to quickly get your career going.

But you can determine how others around you view you by the attitude you display. That doesn't mean you have to think that everything is perfect or that you have to smile when everything seems to be going wrong. It does mean that you need to tackle the job at hand with a positive, can-do attitude. As the old saying goes, "If you think you can or you think you can't, you're right."

Green as the grass in the springtime

So, what is a day in the life of a new appraiser like?

You are likely to be faced with the "everything is new" challenge— from the office to the phone system to the computer system. Given that about 40 percent of real estate appraisers are sole proprietors, you may have the additional challenge of working out of someone's home and having no other office mate than your mentor to ask questions of and emulate. Starting as the single employee of a sole proprietor can be a challenge, as it is oftentimes difficult not to feel like you are intruding.

"Even though you'll probably start at the low end of the totem pole, if you can get by all of the early challenges, it can be the beginning of a wonderful career," says Bob Johnson, managing director of the National Association of Real Estate Appraisers. "Don't get discouraged, hang in there."

On Day 1, your mentor or trainer is likely to give you a general overview of the business and then help you to begin learning the processes.

Smith, who has served as a mentor for several trainees, starts trainees with learning how business comes in and how to log it. "My emphasis in the beginning is to have the trainee learn the workflow."

Appraisal offices normally receive jobs via e-mail or phone call, and it is important that each job gets off on the right foot. That usually means logging the job into some type of system, commonly computerized, so that it is easy to track it through to completion.

Next, you will need to learn the technology required to do the job. Offices can vary from those "early adopters" of technology that receive, process, and return completed appraisals, all via computer, to those that employ manual processes to complete parts of the job.

Most residential appraisers in more urban areas subscribe to at least one database source that provides property sales prices from Multiple Listing Services. These databases are critical to appraisers' ability to value one property against other similar properties (also known as using comparables).

The assignment

Once you've learned the processes and the systems of the appraisal office, you will begin to accompany your mentor on assignments. What does an average residential appraisal entail? A complete basic residential appraisal will take about four hours to complete. Depending on the distance between jobs, appraisers can complete about 10 average residential appraisals per week.

Most assignments come into the appraisal office via electronic form. Once there, the job is logged into a tracking system. At this point the appraiser will learn some basic information about the residence and then seek additional information, often through the town or county clerk's office. In more urban areas, appraisers will be able to gather information such as square footage and perhaps a floor plan electronically, especially for homes in newer subdivisions.

Armed with information about the size of the residence and its location, the appraiser will then begin looking for comparable properties so that he or she can start compiling information about the residence's value.

Often this research is conducted electronically using Multiple Listing Service data of past homes for sale in the area.

The appraiser will then get an appointment to view the property, which can be facilitated by the listing real estate agent (if it involves a property sale). Once on site, the appraiser will measure the building to determine square footage, then take digital pictures of the front and rear of the residence as well as the view from the street. Some appraisers will make a sketch of the building as it sits on the property.

Then, moving inside, the appraiser will view each room, attempting to determine the total value. Some appraisers will sketch a floor plan and take pictures to help them complete the report back in the office.

When taking new trainees out in the field, Smith emphasizes the critical importance of completing detailed drawings of the building being appraised. "It is almost impossible to understand a property if you haven't drawn it very carefully," says Smith. That detailed drawing is also important to the person who hired the appraiser to complete the report. Smith says that during the review of the appraisal report, pages of calculations might be skipped over, but the impression of the report is often based on how well the picture is drawn.

After leaving the residence, the appraiser will drive by the properties identified as comparables, taking pictures and making visual inspections to determine whether they are comparable to the residence being appraised. Next, the appraiser will visit the town or county office to confirm the sales prices of the comparable properties identified (in more rural areas appraisers may need to learn this information from real estate agents, loan officers, or homeowners).

Once back in the office, the appraiser will compile all of the information into the report (often using one of the Fannie Mae forms found in Appendix 6). The digital pictures will be inserted into the report, comparables will be identified, and the report signed and most often sent back in electronic form.

Some appraisers use technology to improve their efficiency during the appraisal, for example by taking notes on a PDA or laptop while viewing the property.

Taking criticism–developing a thick skin

Beginning newspaper reporters commonly wilt under the barrage of criticism inflicted upon them by crusty newspaper editors. It is often the case that an article turned in during the first few weeks on the job returns from the editor's desk with few words untouched. Reporters might receive feedback such as:

- This is a good start, now go fix it.
- OK, it's getting closer, now rewrite it again.
- Are you sure you spelled the mayor's name right?
- Don't you think your article is a little thin on research?

A new reporter may have spent hours agonizing over a 300-word article, taking the time to rewrite it over and over again, only to have an editor run it through the red-penned shredder in mere minutes. The challenges faced by beginning newspaper reporters and appraisers are similar.

As an appraiser trainee, you will probably face constant criticism, and you must prepare yourself for dealing with it. If you're not facing constant criticism, you are either

- Brilliant
- Working for someone who is taking it easy on you

You will need to develop a thick skin and a great attitude. When asked how he felt about failing more than 100 times to develop the incandescent light bulb, Thomas Edison said he hadn't failed—he'd simply found 100 ways that didn't work.

Making mistakes isn't the problem. Not learning from your mistakes is.

Jeff Grendysa, now a successful mortgage banker, says that when he first entered the business he wanted to quit and find another position because of the nearly constant criticism. "You have to learn to live with it," he says.

The one-year mark

As in most careers, most of those who aren't going to make it fail during the first year. You might find out the job isn't for you. The economy might take a dip, and things might get real tight. Or, you just might have found a different calling.

But trainees who have made it to the one-year mark usually find themselves taking on increasingly more complicated work. After a year, trainees will go out on appraisals, do the measuring, and perhaps do the research to find comparables for the report.

By this time, trainees should be making appointments for inspections. In a busy year, you will likely accompany your trainer on 100 or more residential appraisals, and you will begin developing a better understanding of the nuances of residential valuation, including:

- Being fully able to complete an inspection
- Completing a detailed site drawing
- Developing an eye for keen observation with which property valuations are based

The number one problem during the first year is that the trainee doesn't do a good job of balancing variables to select good comparables. This is a skill that can only be developed over time by viewing a large number of properties.

Year two–the big decision

Most trainees attain the 2,000 hours necessary to earn their state appraisal license sometime during their second year. At this time, you may face a decision regarding how to proceed in your career. Choices will include:

1. *Continuing to work for your mentor.* After receiving your license you will qualify for higher pay, so a discussion with your mentor will likely include a determination about whether the business can support another licensed appraiser (you) and whether the trainer/company wants to keep you on. Given the fact that about

40 percent of appraisers are sole proprietors, the chances at this point are that you will be looking either to strike out on your own or locate a job with a larger appraisal company, bank, municipality, etc.

2. *Establishing your own business*. Starting a business is difficult. More than 70 percent of all new businesses fail in their first three years. To improve the odds that your appraisal business won't fail, you will need to start laying the groundwork months in advance. This means first developing a reputation for completing high-quality appraisals on time. If you don't have a solid reputation, only a soaring need for appraisals will help you get off to a strong start. You will also need to start networking as soon as you can to identify places to find appraisal work.

3. *Finding a job with another appraisal company, bank, municipality, etc*. Appraisal jobs are not often listed in newspapers or online job sites. You'll need to network among your peers and other real estate professionals to locate another position well in advance of leaving your trainer.

Five years and counting

Quality appraisers hitting the five-year mark are accomplished real estate appraisers, known for completing high-quality insightful work on time. These quality appraisers constantly challenge themselves to work harder, learn more about their profession, and serve as role models for other new appraisers and trainees.

By now, if you have five years of progressive experience (as opposed to one year of experience five times) you have begun developing a specialty or niche and become an analyst. This niche can provide you with the intellectual stimulation needed to continue growing in the profession. Additionally, this niche also often provides a higher per-hour rate, increasing your income. Because many appraisers choose not to challenge themselves to this degree, the competition for jobs in your niche may be less, providing you with a larger cushion should the economy falter.

You might be a sole proprietor, or perhaps have even begun building your own company with a trainee or two. Should you decide to build your own business, you'll need to spend a substantial amount of time becoming a student of your industry. You'll need to be able to gather information from a variety of sources to get an idea of where the economy is heading in order to determine whether this is a good time to make a go on your own. While no one can predict with 100 percent accuracy the future direction of the economy, you can certainly see if the residential market is dropping or rising, or if office vacancy rates are skyrocketing or holding steady.

This type of information can help you determine your next step, illuminate areas of the appraisal market that may be underserved, and eventually provide you with the type of work and the income you desire.

Once you become a top appraiser and have developed an outstanding reputation and a niche, the need to market yourself and your business will begin to ease. Although at first you may spend a significant part of your week calling banks and mortgage companies, once you learn how to complete more challenging reports you will find that business starts to find you and you have become a valued analyst.

Veterans, professionally growing

While businesses may find those who have established themselves and carved a niche, it is critical not to take your business for granted. Those who do not need to spend a big part of their week prospecting for work must nonetheless make time to stay close to their customers, meeting them informally for breakfast or lunch and not just in a professional setting. Doing this helps the appraiser to form a true partnership, often learning how he or she can be of better service to clients. Those who offer higher levels of service to specific clients usually receive more work from those clients, as well as from others who also network with those clients. Established appraisers' biggest source of new business will likely be referrals, so developing a reputation for professionalism, objectivity, and integrity is critical.

Diversification becomes the key at this stage of your career. You will want to make sure you aren't working for only one or two clients, since you would be too dependent on them. It is difficult to maintain impartiality when working too often for only one client because appraisers are counted on for an unbiased, third-party opinion as to the value of the property.

Wyoming appraiser Anne Johnson, MAI, SRA, says that, not only is it good business sense to expand the number of clients you have, you should also ensure you aren't always working for one type of client. Even though as much as 80 percent of the real estate appraisal business comes from lenders, it is important to find other types of appraisal work, such as work for municipalities, builders, or accountants.

"Be sure you are working for both sides, or you can easily become slanted and not impartial, which is key to the entire profession," says forensic consultant George Dell.

Get into the business now—a conversation with George Dell

Fifteen to 20 years ago, people who were interested in a career in real estate appraising found a job with a savings and loan or bank, received quality training, and their careers were off and running. Today it is a different story, according to George Dell, MAI, SRA, a forensic consultant appraiser based in San Diego, California. "There are no ads in the paper for appraisers anymore," says Dell.

Dell urges those considering the real estate profession to go to college and earn a four-year degree in real estate, finance, math, or statistics, and to have a broad education that includes significant writing experience.

"Ideally you would have some graduate work as well, and then keep your sights on finding a good company and be willing to work for it for cheap," says Dell. "Getting your foot in the door is the trick," he says, adding that appraiser trainees must also work quickly to make themselves valuable to their supervisors and appraisal companies.

Dell, a member of the Appraisal Institute board of directors, says that because of the slowness of the business in the mid-1990s, few people got into the business at that time, and there exists a "gap" in those with significant experience. That can lead to an outstanding opportunity for those entering the business today who are dedicated to working hard to learn how to become a quality real estate appraiser.

Getting his start

Like many appraisers, Dell got into the business as a career changer. For more than 15 years, Dell excelled in the jobs he held; however, they only kept his interest for a short time, and then he was on to a new challenge.

Dell got started in appraising "by accident" in his late 30s as a friend of a friend needed assistance in conducting appraisals. Calling upon the skills he learned earning his accounting degree, Dell went in and out of the business, then finally got back in for the third time. "Then I fell in love with it," he says.

While other jobs he held required him to utilize parts of his skill set at various times, real estate appraising called upon most of his skills, including detailed analysis—something he excels in—as well as people skills and organization skills.

When he entered the business more than 20 years ago, Dell worked hard at marketing to build up his business. He quickly developed an expertise in statistical and econometric analysis, and he began carving out his niche primarily in the southern California market.

He grew his office to a staff of 10 to 15, but an increasing reliance on technology that dramatically reduced the time spent on mundane tasks allowed him to concentrate on analysis, and he eventually opted to work on his own.

Today Dell works primarily in the southern Californian market, but he has also performed residential litigation work throughout the country. Dell specializes in subjective litigation work, including encroachment, condemnation, eminent domain, sewer easements, and view easements.

In California, view easements are a big deal along the coast. It is not uncommon to find properties with a value of $3 million, $1.5 million of which might be attributed to the ocean view. Dell says that view easements are highly valuable and often result in lawsuits, especially when properties change hands.

Specialties are key

Developing a specialty and then continuing to work to be the best in that niche is the way to earn a much higher than average income, says Dell. Those willing to do the type of appraisal work that others aren't doing can earn incomes of $300,000 or more.

Litigation work is an area that pays much higher than average, says Dell, noting that attorneys like to work with appraisers who are also teachers because, in a courtroom, expert witnesses like appraisers are needed to educate the jury and judge.

You win cases with believability, credentials, and how articulate and understandable you are, says Dell, adding that an educated jury working together can display uncommon wisdom.

Deciding to get his MAI and SRA designations were key decisions that helped propel his career. He noted that the designations helped keep his eye on the ethical, professional part of the career rather than on "making a quick buck."

Looking to the future

Dell says that too many real estate appraisers today specialize only in basic home appraisals, not spending the time to develop a sought-after specialty, and are thus vulnerable to economic downturns as well as stiff competition.

To become successful, Dell urges appraisers to continue their educations through organizations such as the Appraisal Institute, American Farm Managers and Rural Appraisers, and the American Society of Appraisers.

As for advice for those looking to enter the profession, Dell says there is a shortage of commercial appraisers specializing in high-end properties. Should the tax laws change so that commercial buildings require appraisals and interim appraisals instead of building depreciation, which is done today, the need for commercial appraisers will increase dramatically.

PART THREE

Choosing a direction

6

Will that be residential, commercial, or both?

This chapter describes why:

- Most appraisers complete both residential and commercial appraisals.
- Smaller territories often mean increased productivity.
- Larger territories mean the appraiser needs strong organizational skills.

There are two basic types of real estate appraisals: *residential,* which covers everything from single-family homes to four-unit homes; and *commercial*, which covers everything from large-scale residential complexes to mom-and-pop stores to "big-box" retail stores to office towers. Most appraisers work on both residential and commercial appraisals.

The average residential appraisal can be completed in a few hours. More complex residential appraisals can take a day or two. The average commercial appraisal will likely take more than a day. More complex commercial appraisals take a week or so. Some of the biggest can take a year or more by a team of appraisers.

Most real estate appraisers enter the business on the residential side for three reasons:

1. Because there are far more residential properties that need appraising
2. Because there are many more residential than commercial appraisers, so when seeking an established appraiser for training/mentoring you will have an easier time finding one
3. Because the average residential appraisal is far less demanding than the average commercial appraisal (and much less time consuming, as noted earlier), making it possible for those new to the profession to become proficient with residential appraisals fairly quickly

Most choose a mix

Most appraisers choose to complete both residential and commercial appraisals. The 2004 Appraisal Institute Member Survey professional profile showed that

- 23 percent specialized in single-family appraisals only.
- 8 percent specialized in commercial appraisals only.
- 21 percent did a mix of residential and commercial appraising (including single-family).
- 48 percent did a mix of residential and commercial appraising (but with no single-family home appraising).

To do both residential and commercial appraising as a sole proprietor can be tough. That's because the average residential appraisal often has a tight deadline. On the other hand, the typical commercial appraisal requires far more detail, can easily take a day or more, and once begun is difficult to interrupt with a residential appraisal that pays far less per hour and may need to be completed quickly.

Deep cycles

Residential appraising is a tough business. The appraiser who chooses to specialize in common residential appraisals may be choosing a difficult career path. That's because residential appraising runs in long, deep cycles of boom and bust.

These deep cycles often result in situations where one year you could be working 16 hours a day and not be able to keep up with the amount of work being sent your way. Then, a year later, you could be scrambling for enough work just to keep you busy.

The bust end of a deep cycle often results in a lack of work for many residential appraisers, especially for those new to the business who have yet to develop a specialty. Appraisal firms do cut staff during these lean times just to survive.

Those choosing to specialize in residential appraising who don't take the time to develop a niche—and therefore qualify for higher-margin jobs—sooner or later may be dealt a tough blow by the economy.

Residential appraisers must be students of the market, networking with real estate professionals and peers to identify segments of the market that are underserved or have growth potential. For example, your research may find lenders looking for an appraiser with a specialty that you have or one that interests you.

Because the industry has a high concentration of appraisers nearing retirement, you also may locate an appraiser who is nearing retirement. This situation could potentially open the door to purchasing that business, or perhaps to a partnership in which you would serve the retiring appraiser's clients going forward. According to the 2004 Appraisal Institute Member Survey, 30 percent of respondents say they are age 55 or older. An additional 34 percent say they are age 45–54.

Although the number of the jobs that will need to be replaced is debatable, the concentration of appraisers who are near retirement does open opportunities.

Home appraisals

The average residential appraisal of a single-family home can pay $200 to $400, depending on the complexity of the appraisal requested and the region of the country. Residential appraisers who employ the latest technology and who concentrate on a small geographic region can turn out several appraisals in a day.

The typical residential appraiser begins with a rather large territory and then, as his or her career progresses, tries to reduce that territory. That's because working in a smaller area reduces the amount of driving between jobs, therefore increasing the appraiser's productivity and raising the per-hour value of an appraisal.

Smaller territories also allow a residential appraiser to have a much better feel for the local real estate market. This can help you to assign a value to the home you are appraising, making it easier for you to determine the best examples to use as comparables in your report to the client.

Determining which houses to use as comparables is a part of the job that those new to the profession find especially challenging. Experienced appraisers are often proficient at understanding home construction and the effect of location on a property's value (for example, a quiet, tree-lined neighborhood with sidewalks versus a similar-looking home on Main Street). Although two houses may look similar on paper, with perhaps nearly the same square footage and number of rooms, an appraiser with an intimate knowledge of additional key information in a town or county will know the difference between neighborhoods (location, location, location), the value of an additional bathroom or an expanded garage, and what a pool will do for resale value.

Geography also has a lot to do with the size of a residential appraiser's territory. In rural North Dakota, an appraiser might need to "specialize" in an area of 100 square miles. This can make the job of the appraiser far more challenging. Rural appraisers tend to wear out their cars much faster, sometimes driving hundreds of miles in a week. Scheduling also becomes critical for rural appraisers, because a rural appraiser with a large territory will need to schedule physical inspections of homes in a logical manner so that he or she isn't driving from one corner of the territory to the other and then back again.

The rural appraiser must also be an expert in determining comparables that may be some distance apart. Rural appraisers will need exceptional people skills that will allow them to befriend other appraisers as well as the local real estate professionals and bankers, who can help them develop their comparables.

Residential appraisers in urban areas often rely on online databases of real estate sales from multiple listing services to find comparables. Urban appraisers will need to learn to sort through the many home sales to determine the best comparables.

As you can see, determining comparables is much different for rural versus urban appraisers: the rural appraiser may have had only a dozen sales in a 100-square-mile territory in the past six months, while the urban appraiser might easily have had a dozen sales in a two-square-mile territory in the past month.

And then there are those residential appraisers who specialize in extremely densely populated areas in major cities. For example, Bruce Kellogg, MAI, managing director at Cushman & Wakefield in Atlanta, Georgia, says some residential appraisers in Manhattan specialize only in co-ops, or condominiums, or brownstone buildings. Kellogg, the 2005 president of the Appraisal Institute, says that because the market is so large, appraisers, depending on their personalities and the direction in which they would like to take their careers, often find themselves professionally attracted to and challenged by a particular type of residential building. Because of the uniqueness and character of these buildings, mortgage bankers, who most often hire appraisers, seek out those appraisers who have developed a specialty in these types of homes and can quickly provide accurate appraisals.

Not as deep

Commercial appraisers don't have the long, deep cycles that characterize the residential appraisal market. But at the same time, the bottom can drop out of the local appraisal market for those who don't diversify their customer base.

For example, if you have decided to specialize in Class A office space, and developers stop building new space, and real estate investors have cooled on the market, there might not be much of a market for your services. However, many commercial appraisers understand market forces and do their best to specialize in areas that react differently to different market conditions.

Anne Johnson, MAI, SRA, who is president of her own appraisal company in Casper, Wyoming, says the commercial market in and around Casper is an energy-based economy, so when fuel prices rise or exploration heats up, appraisers in her region have all the work they can handle. But energy companies are also prone to boom-and-bust cycles, making it essential for appraisers to diversify into different markets.

What can be a challenge for commercial appraisers is a stagnant economy—one characterized by a lack of new development or a dismal economic outlook. If businesses are staying put, developers aren't building, and commercial real estate brokers have little to do, this will likely have a negative impact on the average commercial appraiser as well.

But even when times are tough, there is a need for commercial appraisers. For example, when the economy deteriorates and a company goes out of business, the bankruptcy court still needs to get an accurate determination of the value of the company's real estate holdings. This work is commonly performed by commercial appraisers.

Commercial appraisals

There are far fewer commercial appraisers; therefore there is typically less competition for commercial appraising jobs.

It is difficult to describe the "average" commercial appraisal. In one region it might be the 3,000-square-foot mom-and-pop retail store on Main Street. Other areas might have a higher concentration of suburban office buildings, often averaging 50,000 to 100,000 square feet.

Normally, the different types of commercial properties vary more as the size of the community increases. Communities with fewer than 20,000 residents will probably have a concentration of small retail and office space. In addition to those types of commercial buildings, communities with 20,000 to 75,000 residents will also likely have warehouse space, manufacturing, big-box retail stores, and larger and often more varied office space. (Office space is often characterized as Class A, which is the classiest and often newest buildings, Class B, and finally Class C, which is often the oldest and least-appealing space.)

As with residential appraisals, virtually every commercial appraisal is different because of the wide variety of commercial buildings. In the span of a few weeks, a commercial appraiser might be called on to appraise the value of a 10-year-old convenience store, a 25-year-old small office building, a 60-year-old diner, and a 100-year-old manufacturing building.

What skills are needed to succeed as a commercial appraiser? Anne Johnson says commercial appraisers need to be analytical people who like to dig in deep to review financial statements.

For example, commercial appraisers need to compare income and expenses to similar properties. Is the building being appraised in an area that is above or below average? How strong is its income stream going into the future? Johnson says it is key for commercial appraisers to develop a feel for the local economy and how it can affect the property being appraised.

The average work-week for a commercial appraiser might include working on two different appraisals at a time and visiting properties for on-site inspections. Those in more rural areas will need to find time to network with other appraisers and real estate professionals to anticipate potential changes to the local real estate market. In smaller rural areas, appraisers might also need to network with community economic development professionals, those in the community planning department, and other local business owners to determine if there are changes coming in the community that would affect property values (for example, new developments or plant closings).

When on site, the inspection not only includes the physical condition of the building being appraised, but also whether it is well designed for its use. On site commercial appraisers also need to examine the surrounding neighborhood to review the condition of nearby buildings; determine whether the area is growing, stable, or declining; and then make a determination regarding whether the community will be able to support the commercial enterprise on an ongoing basis.

Jeff Grendysa, SRA, a mortgage banker with a bank based in southeast Michigan, says that bankers need to know the strength of the local economy before deciding whether to offer commercial loans. For example, if a developer proposes that a commercial building be constructed for about $150 per square foot, a banker will want to talk to an appraiser to learn about the local market's supply and demand and to utilize the appraiser's expertise in both analyzing the local market and drawing conclusions about the potential success of the new building. Grendysa says that quality commercial appraisals are extremely valuable to a lender.

What's the difference?

Although residential and commercial appraisers can both develop specialties that enable them to charge higher-than-average fees for their services, there are some basic differences between residential and commercial appraisers.

Residential appraisers often find themselves in more competition with their peers, which tends to keep fees down. Therefore, residential appraisers make more money by being more efficient: being able to complete appraisals faster than their peers, perhaps by developing an efficient work schedule that keeps them in a confined geographic area to minimize travel. Residential appraisers will need to complete several average appraisals a day to make a good living—fewer appraisals if specializing in high-end homes.

Commercial appraisers often enjoy the opportunity to complete appraisals that require more research, more time, and work that draws more heavily on their analytical skills. To determine the value of a commercial building, they not only need to measure it and determine its general condition. They also need to determine its competition, whether the marketplace will be able to continue to support it, and even whether rents are appropriate and whether new buildings might affect the ability to keep tenants at current rates. Also, if investors are looking at similar properties in other towns, they will want to know which will be likely to provide them with a better long-term return on their investment.

Commercial appraisers don't get the satisfaction of completing a job anywhere near as often as residential appraisers, but they can get paid a higher per hour rate.

Reading the crystal ball

So how do you tell where the business growth is today and where it will be going into the future? You must:

- Dedicate yourself to becoming a student of your industry

- Decide to become a student of the region where you work
- Stay involved with your industry
- Join professional associations and serve on their boards (i.e., network)
- Watch for state and national legislation that can affect you.

You must dedicate time every week to developing your business for the long term. Busy appraisers can get caught in the trap of working hard on today's jobs without investing in themselves for the long run.

You need to know what may be coming so that you can respond appropriately. Reacting to events that surprise you can be detrimental to your appraisal career. For example, staying active can help you to learn of a bank merger involving one of your largest clients. You need to know in advance whether the bank you have been working with will be the acquirer, and therefore you may gain additional work, or whether it will be acquired, and perhaps you may be losing a large client. The business world is moving faster every day; to ensure that you keep pace with it, you will need to dedicate yourself to keeping in touch with it.

Not like it used to be

Residential appraisers today face a marketplace that wants reports to be better, faster, and cheaper. Thousands of appraisers across the country serve the loan market, but they are faced with stiff competition and a "better, faster, cheaper" mentality that will likely not change but rather continue to grow more difficult.

To succeed in this market, you will need to embrace new technology that enables you to work faster and more efficiently. The challenge will be that clients will constantly challenge you to do jobs for less and, unless your productivity can increase faster than the price drops, you can face a declining income.

Automated Valuation Models (AVMs) have had a dramatic impact on the least complicated residential appraisals over the past 20 years. Lenders are more likely to use AVMs today to complete appraisals where the risk is low—for example, in refinancings, where the loan-to-value ratio is low.

Forms of AVMs targeted at commercial appraisals in urban settings will probably also begin to chip away at the least complicated part of that market where it is possible to develop comparables.

A fast market in a fast city–a conversation with Julie Burkart

To say that the Las Vegas real estate market has been the place to be for the past decade is an understatement. New casinos on "The Strip" have popped up. Their size and extravagance continue to increase, drawing more tourists and their gaming dollars than ever before, sparking explosive growth in the region.

The strong commercial growth has led to a residential housing boom as tens of thousands of people annually move to the island in the desert for jobs (unemployment is among the lowest in the country) and the consistent warm dry weather.

Since 2000, the Las Vegas residential housing market has seen dramatic appreciation, with median prices for single-family homes topping $300,000 in 2005. Additionally, the number of single-family residences in the market has exploded along with the population, which totals more than 1.4 million.

Property price increases of late have slowed considerably from the breakneck pace of just a few years ago. From 2003 to 2004, single-family home prices in Las Vegas shot up more than 52.4 percent, according to the National Association of Realtors. But that slowdown has brought a market from all-time historic heights down to what is simply a robust market—one in which professionals who serve the real estate market continue to do quite well.

Easy market to work

Among those professionals is Julie Burkart, SRA, president of Southwest Appraisal Service Inc., of Las Vegas. Characterizing the Las Vegas marketplace as an easy one in which to work, Burkart, a residential appraiser, says that the market has some dramatic differences from many others throughout the country.

To begin with, county records include information such as floor plans for most every house in Las Vegas, and many are now available online. While other parts of the country have seen the residential housing stock grow by a few percentage points per year, Las Vegas has experienced double-digit growth during the past 20 years because so much of the housing stock is new. That housing stock has often been built in large subdivisions with large tracts of similar types of houses.

Also, because of the volume of sales, finding good comparables—even in a rapidly appreciating market—often does not require time adjustments.

It is for these reasons that Burkart says the Las Vegas market for residential appraisers is "the easiest in the country," explaining that prior to visiting a property the appraiser can often have a floor plan of the residence faxed to the office or sometimes find it online in the county records.

With so many sales, there are plenty of comparables from which to choose, oftentimes just a block or two away in the same subdivision, says Burkart. Because most residential appraisers can find almost as much work as they would like, those making the highest incomes have spent the time to develop a specialty and have worked within that specialty to increase their productivity.

For example, appraisers working in the same office often divide the Las Vegas region into quadrants so, when inspecting properties, they can look at more than one at a time.

High-end specialty

Burkart specializes in appraising high-end homes and often quotes a two-week turnaround time, providing her the ability to organize her work to maximize effectiveness. She has been working in the market for long enough so that lenders look to her to complete quality reports in a reasonable amount of time. Her company includes a certified residential appraiser, a certified general appraiser, a licensed appraiser, and an intern, who was formerly her office manager.

A former six-year state Commissioner of Real Estate Appraisers for the state of Nevada, Burkart has seen appraising from two sides, both as an appraiser and as the person in charge of handing down punishment for those appraisers who had developed inaccurate reports. The challenge as a commissioner was in determining whether there were violations and, if so, how to handle appraiser punishment fairly, determining whether the appraiser completed poor reports because of improper training or through outright fraud. Making decisions about an appraiser's livelihood was a challenge, she says. Burkart, an appraiser since 1986, also was a residential appraiser in Colorado.

Appraisers today need not succumb to lender pressure to "hit the number" and should report any such pressure to authorities, says Burkart, who also chaired the national continuing education committee for the Appraisal Institute.

As for continuing education, Burkart says the 30 hours every two years required to keep her license in Nevada is enough to keep her and her peers up to date on her profession, provided that courses are selected in order to increase knowledge and not because they are convenient to attend. "Some course offerings are not relevant," she says, adding, "You need to choose wisely."

Continuing education should be supplemented with other industry resources, including reading industry magazines, checking industry Web sites frequently, studying USPAP updates, and keeping active in local chapters of national appraiser organizations, such as the Appraisal Institute.

"It is really important to have connections with other appraisers," says Burkart. "Many appraisers work independently and we need to have someone we can talk to about how to handle different situations that come up and changes that are occurring."

Designations more valuable

Burkart says that industry designations are becoming ever more valuable because some national lenders, concerned with the potential for fraud, are requiring that residential appraisals be completed by those with an SRA designation.

Because residential real estate values continue to rise, becoming one of the key parts of the national's economy, Burkart says she believes that appraisers will continue to play an integral role in residential sales. Because the potential for fraud is very real, she doesn't foresee AVMs cutting deeply into the residential appraiser's livelihood, believing that

mortgage originators need the eyes and expertise that quality appraisers bring to real estate transactions.

As for the Las Vegas market, Burkart says that appraisers moving to the city often can get work fairly quickly. For those looking to enter as a trainee in Las Vegas, Burkart says that those who have integrity and strong writing skills, who can effectively manage their business, and who can clearly communicate can quickly get up to speed and make a living. At the same time, Burkart warns those considering a career as an appraiser to get their educations and intern licenses completed prior to contacting appraisers looking for trainee positions.

Burkart has built her business based on integrity and fulfilling promises made to her clients, so she does not actively search for new clients; rather she spends her time serving her current clients and those clients referred by reputation to the best of her ability.

7

Becoming an analyst

This chapter describes how to:

- Develop a partnership with clients
- Identify in-demand specialties
- Qualify for high-margin work

Most appraisers begin along a similar path—assisting a licensed appraiser with routine tasks—and are often referred to as technicians. But if you would like to earn an above-average income and not be prone to business cycles during which you are working sun up to sun down one year and looking for work to keep you busy the next, you should chart a path to becoming an analyst.

The analyst today is more valued than ever. That's because the markets in which analysts serve are often filled with other professionals who are stretched too thin to anticipate or adequately prepare for changes in those markets.

Analysts not only can help meet their clients' needs of today, but can also help clients plan for tomorrow. It is during this planning stage that analysts position themselves as experts, and in the process create for themselves a stream of work going forward. This is the role in which some of the leaders of the real estate appraisal industry have positioned themselves. You can position yourself in this way as well.

Forming a partnership

Successful real estate appraisal analysts spend the necessary research time to obtain a global view of the changes coming in their markets, make specific recommendations, and carve out a niche that serves them well. And the process doesn't end there. These analysts understand that change is continual, so they not only carve out their niche, but continue to reshape it, evolving from the role of analyst into a true partnership with the clients within the markets they serve.

Appraisers who move into this partnership role don't worry about keeping the lights on or other internally focused concerns. That doesn't mean that once you move into this role you can rest easy. It just means that concerns about marketing and cold calling will likely move off the top of your list of concerns. Replacing these concerns will be staying on top of your game, continuing to study the market, and maintaining your high value to your clients. You will also probably be able to replace your old Chevy with a new Cadillac. Sounds simple, and the concept is. Of course, getting there isn't simple or everybody would be doing it. It is far easier to focus only on today, take in as much work as makes sense, and worry about changes as they come along. That is certainly the approach taken by some appraisers, but the experts interviewed for this book all agree: change can come rapidly, sometimes with no warning, and you can go from a booming business in which you struggle to keep up with the volume of work to one in which you need to do cold calling just to keep busy.

Experts agree—the analyst role is the way to go. Make up your mind and chart your path beginning today.

The way to go

As you can see, in either residential or commercial real estate appraising, your best route to making more money and increasing job security is by increasing your productivity and becoming an analyst. How?

1. Research the needs of the local market.
2. Then carve out a niche that is highly valued in your local market.
3. Then use the correct technology to do your job faster.

That doesn't mean that you completely abandon more basic types of appraisals. It does mean that your goal is to become less reliant upon the economy and the more basic appraisals and to take more control in determining your level of income. Your goal is to become an analyst who partners with professionals in the market or markets in which you have chosen to serve.

Although not everyone is cut out to be an early adopter of the latest technology, if you are involved in your profession and network among your peers, you can find out how the latest technology helps them do their work more efficiently. Software that is designed to improve your efficiency, helping you do everything from handling tasks such as inserting a flood map into your residential report to helping you to write a comprehensive 50-page narrative for a commercial property with several unique characteristics, will help you to complete reports faster and at a higher level.

Making better use of your time also means developing systems in your office for handling routine tasks quickly and efficiently so that you can spend more time on the parts of your business that earn you the greatest financial reward. Running an office efficiently is an art, one that can be constantly honed to make sure you are completing routine tasks as quickly as possible.

Work on your business

You must be sure to spend some time every week working on your business, not simply doing appraisals. What does this mean? Basically, it means that while working on appraisals will keep the lights on today, if you aren't spending some time planning for tomorrow, the lights might not be on for too long. Some residential appraisers who specialized exclusively in the simplest residential real estate appraisals saw much of their work disappear with the advent of AVMs, while other appraisers who quickly embraced technology and are able to complete a higher level of appraisals in a fraction of the time are doing quite well for themselves.

The last thing you want to do is to become a dinosaur, only reacting to change after it happens—often too late for the marketplace. Instead, you need to do what the leaders of the industry do: be a student of the marketplace, respond to changes as you see them, and move yourself from being a mere technician into an analyst role, providing valued consultation.

In most industries, the professional who evolves from technician to analyst is more highly valued, is able to charge a much higher hourly rate, and has a greater chance of being able to earn a good living. Appraisers are no different. Find an appraiser earning an above-average income, and more often than not you've found a successful analyst.

High demand

Carving out a niche—preferably one in which there is little competition but significant demand—can help you earn more. For example, the average single-family home residential appraisal in the Detroit area pays $250 to $300. But a residential appraiser with advanced education and skill who develops a relationship with a tax law firm could gain referrals to well-heeled clients with substantial residences who are unhappy with their property tax bills and would pay $6,000 to $8,000 for a quality appraisal report.

To qualify for this sort of high-paying work, appraisers will probably need an advanced degree. The level of accountability for such high-margin work is high, and appraisers need to be comfortable with providing court-room testimony if necessary. Attorneys tend to prefer appraisers who are also teachers.

Talk with top appraisers

One secret to success is to spend significant time talking with appraisers who are higher on the pyramid than you are. Some of this success is bound to rub off, and you'll learn how to climb higher. Just remember, the higher you travel up the pyramid, the more work you'll need to do to get there and stay there. But the view from the top is much better.

Networking should begin with professional appraisal organizations in the region in which you live. Getting involved with other industry leaders gives you the opportunity to talk with and learn from other appraisers who share common interests and may be working in markets that interest you. Veteran appraisers often learn the tricks of the trade the hard way, and wise newcomers learn from the veterans' mistakes and emulate their best practices.

Getting involved doesn't mean you have a membership, rarely go, or get to meetings late and leave early. Getting involved means just that— not only being a member, but serving on the board or on committees that interest you, so that you can learn new concepts while giving back to your profession to make it better (better for others and for you).

The first time you meet an appraiser at a function, he or she will not be likely to provide you with the keys to his or her success. But getting to know other appraisers on a personal level by serving in leadership positions and meeting with them during informal occasions will allow you to learn valuable information that can help shape your growing career. And you'll be volunteering your time to improve your industry at the same time.

Questions to ask

Virtually everyone likes to talk about themselves and how they have gotten to where they are today in their careers. When meeting with appraisers at industry meetings, ask questions such as:

- How did you get started in the appraisal business?
- What types of appraisals did you first complete?
- What kind of appraisal work do you do today?

- Are you developing any new specialties?
- Where do you see the industry heading?
- If you were me, what are the steps you would take to build a successful career?
- Who else should I talk with about their successful careers?

Asking these sort of open-ended questions will provide you with a great opportunity to learn from top appraisers serving your local market. They can also provide you with valuable insight into changes in the market that can help you to chart your path to success.

Appraisers specialize in all types of residential and commercial development. A partial list follows.

Some residential specialties

- High-end residential homes
- Condominiums
- Co-ops
- Brownstone buildings
- Modular homes
- Manufactured homes
- Old homes
- Homes in planned unit developments

And there are other types of specialties that include divorces, right-of-way disputes, and valuation for estate planning.

Some commercial specialties

- Suburban office complexes
- Gas stations
- Office condominiums
- Convenience stores
- High-rise office buildings
- Shopping malls
- Strip malls
- Campgrounds

- Golf courses
- Hotels
- Restaurants
- Marinas
- Bars
- Resorts

Additional education

With any of these specialties you will probably need additional education. Some of that education can be earned while you are completing your continuing education requirements to retain your license. When talking with your peers about their specialties, be sure to ask them about the courses they took and how they gathered the expertise necessary to be viewed as a valued expert.

The world is growing smaller with every day. When national companies are seeking to build stores, gas stations, or hotels they often look for local appraisers with specialties in the specific type of business they are building. Spending the time to educate yourself in your specialty and becoming an expert in that specialty will help you to get more business from companies based in your area, as well as national chains.

Many of the top appraisers interviewed for this book first started out by carving a niche in a specific type of appraisal. Then they continued to listen to their customers and increased their value by providing customers with the type of reports they needed.

Top appraisers begin their career similarly and continue to evolve their skills to better serve their clients. In doing so, they go from being technicians, who are viewed simply as vendors, to analysts, who become valued professional members of the team.

Other organizations

In addition to becoming an involved member in a professional real estate appraisal organization and taking additional education, you should also consider being active in a local professional real estate organization. This will allow you to learn more about the local real estate market, helping you to identify trends as they begin to emerge rather than waiting to read about them in the newspaper several months after the trend is in full swing (and often past its peak). Real estate organizations also provide you with access to people who will need your services. And by becoming a member and, once again, getting involved on the board or a committee, you show your willingness to give back.

Getting involved will take time that you could be using to complete appraisals and make more money today. But if you decide that you want to be in this profession for the long haul, you need to position yourself in your market and among your peers as a leader—the type of professional whom others look to for valuable insight—and you will need to spend time planning for the long term. Additionally, you will become the type of professional who is looked up to and called upon as an expert analyst in the area in which you specialize.

Along with being active in professional organizations, you will need to take the requisite continuing education every year to keep your real estate appraisal license. Make sure that your continuing education is calculated to stretch your mind to new possibilities, rather than simply refreshing what you already know over and over.

Professional designations

As the market continues to mature, many appraisers are spending the time necessary to qualify for professional designations. Although it is true that some parts of the real estate appraisal market do not value professional designations, earning a designation is a sign of professionalism and helps you position yourself as someone who has devoted a significant amount of time to furthering your education and is concerned about acquiring the background necessary to complete more complex appraisals. Also, in today's global marketplace, having a designation after your name can give you an advantage over other appraisers in the marketplace. All things being equal, appraisers with designations are more highly recognized than those without them. And for those moving into more complex appraisals, especially those in commercial appraising, a designation can make an important difference. Two of the most common designations—the SRA and MAI—are awarded by the Appraisal Institute.

In addition, being a member of the Appraisal Institute, the National Association of Real Estate Appraisers, or another professional appraisal organization that is active in your region affords you access to resources such as publications, libraries, study groups, and referral programs that can be invaluable as you progress in your career.

Even when you are busiest—perhaps facing a huge time crunch—and are unable to allocate time to local appraisal or real estate functions, you can often find bits of time at night or over the weekend to keep up by reading the latest real estate publications, visiting Web sites, or calling your peers to keep in touch. The key is to stay current and not become detached from the trends of your industry for long periods of time.

What's next?

So you are licensed, involved with the local chapter of a national appraisal industry group and a local real estate group, and have a professional designation or two. What's next?

Well, for those who continually look to move further up in the market, getting involved with your appraisal organization on the state and national levels is a next logical step. While getting involved locally plugs you into local happenings, moving up to the state and national levels can provide you with valuable insight into trends on the macro level that will eventually shape your local market.

Again, this will require a time commitment on your part, but it will be justified as you begin charging a higher hourly rate. A new affiliation on the state or national level can help provide you with the opportunity to collect more information to better serve your market as an analyst and business partner.

Giving back

By this time, you are reaching the top of your game. Your reputation is strong in the local market. You are called upon to provide your expertise in the area in which you specialize. You are recognized both by your peers and those for whom you work as the person they want to partner with. And your income is rising as you are called upon to provide your expert analysis in more complex areas. What is your next goal?

Think back to when you first entered the business. Were there one or two people who helped shape your career? Now, as a leading professional, you can look back and see that those who helped you find your way also helped strengthen the industry. Could it be your turn to repay the favor?

Serving as a mentor can be challenging, but at the same time it can be quite rewarding. You will be giving your knowledge and expertise to someone just entering the business and will teach them why being an appraiser with the highest ethical standards will help the entire profession raise its image.

You will need to spend considerable time to identify a candidate who will fit with your personality and the type of work that you do. You need to find someone with the appropriate skill set who can learn quickly. In fact, bringing on the right person can help you to concentrate your energies on more of the high-margin work that you might be dabbling in.

At first it will be difficult and time-consuming to get this new person up to speed. But if you have done your homework when selecting this candidate (perhaps someone you met at a local professional appraisal meeting), the relationship can give your career a boost and provide you with the satisfaction of knowing you helped someone enter the business, much like the way you received a hand to get your career started.

A new recruit can provide you with a fresh set of eyes with which to look at your work and may help you reach new heights, perhaps through business contacts new to your office. And there is nothing like the enthusiasm a new recruit can bring to an office. In the eyes of a new appraiser, nothing is standard, nothing is routine. Everything is new and exciting.

If you manage an office of appraisers, might there be one or two who are stuck in a rut and could benefit from the fresh enthusiasm and energy of having a new face around? Nobody wants to lag at the bottom of the pecking order for long. If you have hired quality candidates, all will be looking to improve their skills—and who wants the "new guy" to be getting all of the attention and praise?

Opportunities abound for appraisers–
a conversation with Bruce Kellogg

Bruce Kellogg, MAI, is an unabashed proponent of the real estate appraisal profession, taking every opportunity to speak about the opportunities that present themselves for those looking to join the profession. The 2005 president and chairman of the Appraisal Institute (AI) board of directors, he oversaw a promotional campaign during his tenure at the helm of the AI that was aimed at raising the profession's public image. Hopefully this will lead to more opportunities for appraisers to work as consultants with other professionals, such as lawyers and accountants, as well as attracting high-quality candidates.

Beginnings

Kellogg entered the appraisal profession shortly after graduating from college. There was an opening in the bank for which he was working. So he inquired, received encouragement from his father who had always wanted to get into real estate, "…and 33 years later, here I am."

Kellogg quickly gravitated toward working on commercial appraisals because he found the diversity in the types of businesses he appraised and the scope of that part of the business to be especially challenging.

Currently a managing director for Cushman & Wakefield in Atlanta, Georgia, Kellogg got his start in New York City, where he quickly got involved in the business, networking with nationally prominent real estate appraisers who taught him the importance of continuing his education. He credits Jim Gibbons, whom he called one of the giants in the industry, with clearly explaining capitalization and how real estate is simply another form of investment, competing with stocks and other types of investments. "Jim was—and still is—a real icon of the industry," says Kellogg.

During 2005, Kellogg's duties as head of the AI provided him with the opportunity to travel across the country, speaking to industry groups and representing the industry to members of the press. He has long been active in the business, serving since 1990 on the AI board through the mid-1990s, and, in 1996, as the president of the Atlanta Area AI chapter.

"I believe if you give of yourself, you get back many times over," says Kellogg. "You don't give to get, you get when you give for the right reasons."

The director of quality control for the Valuation Services division at Cushman & Wakefield, responsible for ensuring that appraisal templates are accurate and meet the highest professional standards, Kellogg has conducted random audits of appraisals by his firm across the country. It is his job to go into company branch offices and sit down with a group of appraisers, provide them with a summary of what he found in the reports, then sit down with individual appraisers for an hour or two each to provide constructive feedback.

Kellogg says his job is not to criticize, but rather to encourage appraisers, giving them the tools to write better reports and better communicate with their clients so that surprises are avoided whenever possible.

Entering the business

The biggest challenge faced by new college graduates just beginning the real estate appraisal profession is developing the discipline to do the job correctly. Because this doesn't necessarily need to be a "9-to-5" job, appraisers need to develop self-discipline and project an image that exudes professionalism and integrity.

When he started out in the profession, Kellogg wore a jacket and tie at work every day, projecting a professional image that was both recognized and remembered.

Kellogg says that career changers entering the business may find the proper use of technology to be challenging, as they attempt to quickly get up to speed and use it to improve their efficiency.

It is essential for anyone entering the business to find a quality mentor and to learn as much as possible, as quickly as possible. Kellogg says that many mentor/trainee relationships provide both with an opportunity to develop a friend and trusted professional colleague who provides referral business and the opportunity to capitalize on each other's strengths.

Looking forward

Kellogg sees great opportunity for appraisers at all levels who embrace technology and continue to improve their efficiency. "You have to be flexible in order to adapt to changes," he says, adding that appraisers all across the country, in both urban and rural settings, face constant change.

With auto makers building new manufacturing facilities in rural Alabama and Tennessee, and not in places like Detroit or Dallas, the global economy is extending its reach into rural and less-populated areas today and will continue to expand its reach tomorrow and the next day. "If rural appraisers think they aren't going to be impacted by the global economy, they are missing the boat," says Kellogg. "The world is shrinking and there is more international business than ever before."

Kellogg encourages all appraisers to continue their educations and to strive for professional designations to improve their image in the marketplace. "The vast majority of those who have adopted technology have improved their salaries," he says, adding that a survey conducted by the AI shows that those with an SRA professional designation earn an average of 26 percent more, or $13,000 annually, than other residential appraisers. The 1999 study reported that SRAs had an average gross income from real estate activities of $94,049 versus $68,614 for other residential appraisers.

8

Become the appraiser everyone wants to hire

This chapter describes why:

- Writing outstanding narratives is a key to success.
- Many appraisers choose to become sole proprietors.

So, how do you become an appraiser that everyone wants to hire? It's not easy. But as discussed previously, the higher up the pyramid you climb, the better the view, the less competition you'll have, and the better the chance to earn an income that is well above the average for an appraiser.

Success in the appraisal business won't be handed to you. Achieving success requires that you dedicate yourself to

- Hard work
- The highest level of integrity
- Providing the level of service the client wants—and perhaps a little bit more

- Including everything in your reports that your clients will need
- Sometimes serving as a consultant to help clients understand the level of appraisal they need
- Sometimes saying "No" if your schedule doesn't permit you to complete high-quality work in the time frame the client expects

The experts interviewed for this book agree that reaching the top of the profession requires more than simply being a good appraiser. As we've discussed, it is the appraiser who grows from a simple form-filling technician to an analyst who eventually reaches the higher levels of the profession.

Writing outstanding narratives

Narratives that are outstanding break down the complex into easy-to-understand terms that the client has no trouble following. Writing is one part of the job that is often overlooked by those considering the profession. They believe that only strong mathematical and analytical skills are necessary for success.

But to succeed at higher levels of both residential and commercial appraising (and to earn a higher rate of pay), the narrative portion of the report becomes by far the most important part. Higher levels of the profession often call for review of high-value properties, often with unique features, requiring a high level of analytical skill. These more complex reports require appraisers to pull in large quantities of data to make an accurate valuation determination. The detailed data can result in confusing written reports unless the appraiser spends the time necessary to break the information down into a logical, easy-to-follow narrative.

What types of work can appraisers look forward to as they move their careers forward? Most appraisers begin by valuing land and improvements. Some then choose to move on to:

- Reviewing appraisals
- Consulting on real estate transactions
- Determining eminent domain
- Providing expert testimony

- Resolving *ad valorem* taxation issues
- Evaluating businesses
- Evaluating contaminated property

Off on your own

Taking your career to new heights may include, as it does for many, starting your own business. For those who are on their own, the benefit most often noted is the ability to make your own hours when you are your own boss.

What those new to running their own businesses often don't realize about those flexible hours is that, while you gain the ability to spend time watching your children play sports in the afternoon, that time will have to be made up, often at night and over weekends. And given that you are now in charge, if a client calls requesting a rush job on a Friday afternoon at 3:00, guess who will miss her tee time?

Top appraisers who successfully run their own businesses start with integrity as their cornerstone. But to succeed on an ongoing basis, you will need to spend considerable time marketing your talents.

Your marketing time will likely consist of:

- Visiting your clients to determine their needs and to inquire about additional work
- Networking with peers in statewide organizations so that you can develop a network of appraisers who can assist you
- Networking with others in the real estate industry (including mortgage bankers, financial planners, and attorneys) who can send additional work your way and who can serve as valued advisors

Going off on your own also carries costs with it. These costs include office space, unless you decide to work out of your own home; computers and software; other office equipment, including a fax machine, desks, phones, etc.; and insurance, including health insurance for you and your dependents, as well as business insurance. As the owner of your business, other costs may include professional organization fees, networking costs, and the cost to maintain your license.

The increase in the number of online database sources of real estate sales information is making it easier for appraisers to base their businesses in their homes. While in the past 20 years some appraisers may have chosen to pay for professional office space, the reverse of that is often true today, especially for residential appraisers. Appraisers can now get reports via e-mail, complete reports using software, search a database to gain comparable information, add digital photos to the report, and then e-mail a .pdf file of the report back to the client.

Sole proprietors, always a large percentage of the industry, will likely continue to comprise the majority of appraisers.

A unique market–a conversation with Dave Munsell

On November 21, 1620, the Pilgrims first landed in North America at what is now Provincetown, Massachusetts, at the tip of Cape Cod. They first met the Native Americans farther down the Cape, at what is now called First Encounter Beach in Eastham. Most people know the Pilgrims settled in Plymouth, sailing down from Cape Cod into calmer waters.

What does all of this have to do with real estate appraisers?

Well, given that the Cape Cod area was among the first areas settled in the United States, it means that some of the housing stock is the oldest in the country. And given that Baby Boomers are buying everything near the water they can, especially in scenic areas, the Cape Cod housing market, which has seen rapid appreciation over the past 20 years, has everything from houses that are more than 300 years old to ones under construction as you read these words.

This means that appraising homes on Cape Cod is a big challenge for three reasons:

1. Because some of the housing stock is so old, appraisers need to be able to determine the value of very old homes, many of which have unique characteristics—and unique challenges to repair them.

2. Because the old housing stock is often next to homes that may be only 50, 25, 10 years old, or under construction, it can be challenging for appraisers to determine value.
3. And, like many beachfront communities, proximity to the water and whether the home has a water view is critical to determining its value.

The Cape Cod market is also one in transition. In many parts of the United States, residents who are just starting out buy smaller, less expensive homes. As their incomes grow and their need for space increases, they trade up to larger homes. And some people trade up a third time, purchasing homes that may have values in the top 10 percent of that community's housing stock.

But because of rapid home value appreciation over the past 20 years, some people are choosing to "cash out" of their smaller homes or cottages and take the proceeds to purchase places in less expensive communities near the water farther down the Eastern seaboard, often in the Carolinas. Smaller homes or cottages that 20 years ago might have been worth about $50,000 can be worth $300,000 to $450,000 or more today.

Market in transition

Dave Munsell, owner of Munsell Appraisal Services, Inc., of Marston Mills, Massachusetts (located on Cape Cod), says another change in the Cape housing market is that more people than ever before are buying properties for use as second homes. Not only are those second homes smaller seasonal cottages of about 1,000 square feet, but also larger homes of 2,000 to 3,000 square feet, or even larger.

The housing transition under way on Cape Cod makes it challenging for real estate appraisers to keep up with the market. Munsell, who has about a dozen appraisers working as independent contractors for his agency, says it is virtually impossible for one appraiser to provide accurate values for properties throughout Cape Cod and the islands of Martha's Vineyard and Nantucket.

That's because identical houses in adjacent towns can have very different values. Within the towns, proximity to the highway can also have a big impact. And then there is the proximity to the water—a 1,500 square foot house on Cape Cod Bay might be worth $1 million if it is on the beach and $400,000 or less if it is three-quarters of a mile from the water.

Appraisers on the Cape do have sales data with which to determine comparables, but that is only a start. The Cape Cod appraiser needs to have much more information, such as how close to the water a house is; whether the beach it is closest to is more or less desirable than others in the area; if it is near other landmarks that can increase its value (such as the Cape Cod Rail Trail, a 25-mile-long paved bicycle path).

Because there are so many variables when developing comparables, it isn't uncommon for Munsell's staff to look at 15 to 20 comparables prior to narrowing them down to three.

Appraisers in Munsell's agency complete some 2,000 to 3,000 appraisals in an average year, ranging from small condominiums worth less than $200,000 to mansions worth $15 million or more. The work can be seasonal, with the spring and fall the busiest times, as winters on the Cape can be desolate, and during the summer many homes are rented to vacationers.

Each of the appraisers in Munsell's company specializes in just one or two towns, providing them the opportunity to develop their expertise. They put together their own personal databases of sales information, which helps them to increase their productivity. Munsell and his appraisers make paired sales analyses of recent sales, doing the research necessary to determine whether a sale was a typical arm's-length transaction, or whether circumstances changed the value of the home either upwards or downwards.

Become a good appraiser

The goal is to become a good—not just an adequate—appraiser, says Munsell, adding that his clients understand the value of having appraisers that specialize in a specific geographic area.

"Good clients want you to do the work for them and they trust your judgment," says Munsell, adding, "I'd much rather have 10 good clients than 15 "iffy" clients." For example, Munsell tries to work on two to three appraisals at a time when working on Nantucket because he flies there.

Fog can ground planes, and a mortgage banker who doesn't understand the Cape market might penalize him for not getting to the appraisal on time when someone who understands the market might not do so.

Bank consolidation has caused several of his clients disappear, but due to Munsell's reputation for quality, the business remains strong, growing from about four appraisers six years ago to a dozen in 2005, along with a business partner. That reputation for quality can lead to referrals—for example, from real estate agents to banks and mortgage companies and to residents seeking a value on their homes.

Munsell says that while mortgage bankers often look to get the highest appraised value possible, the quality bankers understand that appraisers are just doing their jobs when completing a quality appraisal, and they will use their services again, even if the appraiser doesn't value the property as high as they would have liked.

Noting that he has fired clients that have consistently applied too much pressure, Munsell says he does much of his work today for banks. He does no marketing for new clients, but works to ensure that all appraisals are completed on time and to the highest standards. Communications with your clients is key, says Munsell, adding that you can lose your integrity quickly.

Coming from a family of entrepreneurs who have run a variety of companies on the Cape, Munsell has been an appraiser since 1984. With a young family, he was eager to get out of his family-owned construction company. He sought out a single-proprietor appraiser and went to work for him.

The Cape Cod market may be changing, but Munsell says that his competition remains steady, not only from other appraisers based on Cape Cod, but also from other firms looking to gain a foothold in the market. The key to growing his firm in a market in which the average cost of appraisals has been flat over the past 10 years is having appraisers who understand local markets and can efficiently and quickly complete quality reports.

High-end specialty

Munsell's specialty is high-end homes, many of which are located on Nantucket, an exclusive island just south of Cape Cod. Munsell says he works on about 8 to 10 properties of $10 million or more on Nantucket every year; and about five each on Martha's Vineyard and Cape Cod.

"I shake my head every time I go out there," says Munsell about Nantucket, a market that has seen property value increases of 10 to 20 percent annually for the past several years.

As an example of the rapid appreciation on Nantucket, Munsell says a property appraised for $215,000 in 1991 went under contract in 2005 for $1.5 million.

Appraisers new to the Cape Cod market are always challenged to learn the difference in property values between towns, within towns, and of same-sized homes of different eras.

Mentoring about 15 trainees during his career, Munsell says that those who succeed often come to the business with a background in real estate and have lived in the area for a long time, have good analytical skills, are willing to learn, and are organized and know how to use their time effectively.

The last point is especially critical for appraisers, many of whom are attracted to the business by the flexibility the job offers. Appraisers have the ability to set their own hours, often completing reports when their schedule permits—for example, at night or on weekends. Additionally, since many appraisers work out of their own homes, they must be self-starters who are disciplined to get the job done on time and to the highest standards.

"You need to be able to close the door and get to work," says Munsell about those who, like himself, work out of their homes, adding that you need a separate space in your home to set up your office.

9

You've made it!

This chapter describes why:

- Regularly spending time working on your business is critical.

- Getting involved outside the office helps grow your business.

- Understanding the importance of continuing education is essential to success.

So you found yourself a mentor, completed the 2,000 hours, passed the licensing exam, made it through the gauntlet of the first few years, and now you are looking for some smooth sailing in your career.

Making it this far means that you have worked hard, and you rightly deserve to take a look to see how far you have come, pat yourself on the back, and perhaps indulge yourself in some type of tangible reward. But don't spend too much time celebrating, because tomorrow will be here before you know it, and along with it comes continual change and new challenges to confront.

Like most businesses today, the real estate appraisal business doesn't stand still. It is being revolutionized by technology. It seems like only yesterday when appraisals were completed the "old fashioned" way: primarily with a pencil and paper, to which you added photographs that would take days to be developed, and the U.S. Postal Service to send jobs back and forth.

Today, the business is highly computerized and jobs are commonly e-mailed back and forth. More change is most certainly on the way. And while you have been busy carving your niche in the appraisal business, others have been entering the business, some of them with an eye on the very niche you currently occupy.

That doesn't mean you should circle the wagons to protect your niche, nor does it mean you should abandon it. But you should be looking constantly for underserved portions of the real estate appraisal business that may need first-class professionals like yourself to serve it better. How do you do that?

As we've already discussed in Chapter 7, it's important to spend time working on your business. Be a student of the marketplace, respond to changes as you see them, and position yourself on the path to becoming an analyst. Be sure to carve out your niche, but continue to reshape it, and try to enter into a true partnership with the clients you serve. Don't focus only on today, but plan for the future growth of your business.

Being a student of your local market conditions can help position you as the expert that your peers, other professionals, and perhaps reporters from your local newspaper will want to speak with.

For example, perhaps you are an appraiser who has carved out a niche in mid- and high-end residential appraisals in a three-town area. To get an idea of where the local housing market may be heading, you may want to follow these five indicators.

1. One leading indicator of future home prices is the length of time that houses are on the market. You can easily track this indicator using multiple listing data readily available to you.

    You will find that when houses are quickly moving on and off of the market, it means that the market is hot, and demand is likely outstripping supply. Over the long run, when demand outstrips supply, prices increase.

Of course, as prices increase, this can lead to more people putting their homes on the market as they attempt to lock in big profits. Growing families might be looking to trade up to a larger home, while empty nesters might be considering trading down to a smaller home or to a lower priced and/or warmer region.

And when houses stay on the market for a longer time, that often is an indicator that prices will likely moderate, and if the trend increases over a period of months—or when the length suddenly and rapidly increases—it can lead to a decline in home prices.

2. Another piece of information that can help you to determine future pricing is consumer confidence, another leading economic indicator. Consumer confidence is a predictor of consumer spending on everything from clothing to cars to homes. It is an indicator covered in the business section of almost every daily newspaper and is widely reported on in various online sources.

 When consumer confidence increases or holds steady at a high rate, it generally helps to support the housing market. People who are confident about the future direction of the economy are more likely to be active buyers, helping to support higher home prices. Of course, the opposite is also true: when consumer confidence drops, it can often lead to a softer housing market in which prices stop increasing, and can actually decrease.

3. Of course, a big factor in the housing market is current mortgage rates. While 30-year mortgage rates plummeted to 40-year lows in 2003, they have since increased, but still remain historically low (30-year rates were more than 9 percent in January 1995). But rapidly increasing mortgage rates can have a dampening affect on a slowing housing market, as consumers can only afford a smaller house for the same monthly payment. Additionally, should mortgage underwriters begin taking a more conservative route to writing some of the creative mortgage products which have proliferated over the past few years, those with poor credit could get squeezed out of the market, and cut overall housing demand.

4. A lagging indicator that often helps to influence consumer confidence is the unemployment rate. Trends in the unemployment rate are often as important as the level of unemployment, as a sudden increase or decrease in the unemployment rate will affect home values.

   As a lagging indicator, by the time the unemployment rate shows a substantial move (for example, a half point) in either direction, a trend in housing prices is often already established. Nonetheless, the unemployment rate can often provide clues as to the strength of the current trend, as several months of an improving employment market can boost consumer confidence, and move potential home buyers into action.

5. Finally, keeping an eye on the overall direction of housing values in your region can help you to learn how the above four indicators influence the housing market today, and can help you spot trends as you become a veteran market watcher.

This is just one example of how you can become an expert appraiser who spends time becoming a student of the market and can respond appropriately to it, rather than reacting to structural changes that have already occurred.

Of course you'll also want to continue to network with professional appraisal organizations, other appraisers, and local real estate organizations. Get as involved as possible. Being seen as a leader among your peers will greatly benefit you, and people will turn to you for your advice and expertise. And of course, keep up with your continuing education. This is required to keep your appraisal license, but is also a great opportunity to stretch your mind to new possibilities.

Consider spending the time to qualify for professional designations. Two of the most common, the SRA and MAI, are awarded by the Appraisal Institute. It is also a good idea to become a member of the Appraisal Institute, the National Association of Real Estate Appraisers, or other professional appraisal groups that are active in your area. These memberships will give you access to invaluable resources, including publications, libraries, study groups, and referral programs.

Finally, now that you've made it, you should consider serving as a mentor. This is your chance to repay the favor your mentor did for you when you were just getting started. It's also a great opportunity to help a bright new trainee get off on the right foot and to revitalize your business with a fresh perspective and renewed energy.

A great profession for women–a conversation with Anne Johnson

There is great potential for women who are detail oriented to become high-quality appraisers, says Anne Johnson, MAI, SRA, who is president of her own appraisal company in Casper, Wyoming.

Being your own boss means you can increase the flexibility of your schedule, often deciding what hours you are going to work to complete the job at hand. "It is kind of exciting to be on your own," says Johnson, adding that you have the ability to take a day or afternoon off to follow your children's sports activities.

Appraising runs in her family, as Johnson's husband is also an appraiser with an MAI designation from the Appraisal Institute. Anne quickly moved toward commercial appraisals, and she has been running her own company for more than 18 years. "Sometimes I wish I had paid holidays," she jokes.

Rural Wyoming

Because Wyoming is a rural state—the largest city has only 55,000 residents—Johnson has handled a variety of commercial work, including light industrial, retail, motels, some larger subdivisions, and right-of-way work. "Personally I like to do more complicated properties," says Johnson.

Based on how well the energy sector is performing, Johnson has seen the state's boom-and-bust economy at the top and bottom and has managed to develop a strong business. Her business is based on strong networking and interpersonal skills that are critical to getting both clients and the information necessary to get the job done. Johnson explains that appraisers in rural areas need strong interpersonal skills because if you don't develop rapport with local officials—such as town clerks, development directors, real estate brokers, and even the owners of businesses—you won't be able to do your job. Part of the reason for that to be true is that Wyoming is a nondisclosure state, meaning that real estate sales prices aren't recorded in the county courthouse.

Rural appraisers often spend more time completing assignments than do their urban counterparts, since you need to collect more data using personal rather than electronic sources. Working all over the state, but concentrating in a 250-mile radius from her home, Johnson works closely with local experts to learn about comparable sales that she uses to complete her reports. Writing reports in Wyoming can be challenging because the economy can move up and down quickly, resulting in rapidly fluctuating prices.

With 160,000 miles on her five-year-old car, Johnson spends quite a bit of time behind the wheel, but manages to do so in an efficient manner, scheduling site visits effectively and spending time while in a town to gather as much recent sales information as possible. She spends about three to four nights per month away from home.

As the only female MAI in Wyoming, Johnson is sometimes met with preconceived notions, but she has overcome those notions with her professionalism and ability to develop high-quality appraisal reports.

Her reputation has grown to the point today that she has as much work as she needs and does not market her practice to generate additional work.

Continuing education

People who go the extra mile by continuing their educations will likely go the extra mile in completing detailed reports, says Johnson, who notes that designations show the marketplace that you take your profession seriously.

Although it is challenging to get started in the real estate appraisal profession, Johnson says that those with an analytical ability who like to dig deep into financial statements and who are good writers can succeed. "But you also need to network with your peers," she says.

"If you are always expanding your abilities and are willing to do the difficult tasks that others might not be willing to do, the appraisal profession offers solid opportunities," she says.

"Real estate appraisal is a challenging profession because the real estate market is so dynamic—always changing. This and the opportunity to talk with investors and owners about their businesses and insights are what make this career interesting to me. There's seldom a dull moment," she says.

PART FOUR

External forces changing the profession

10

Appraisers play key roles in society

This chapter describes:

- How to handle pressure to "hit the number"
- Where to turn for help when the pressure is on
- When to consider firing a client

*T*he property has been on the market for six months. The listing broker has made numerous appointments to show it. A lot of people have come through to "kick the tires." But no bids.

Then an out-of-town broker gets involved. She brings over someone who finds the property to be exactly what she is looking for. A bid is placed. A counteroffer is made. A counter to that offer is made. Finally a price is settled upon.

The prospective owner contacts a mortgage broker. They settle on the terms of the loan, and a loan application is made.

The listing broker very much wants this deal to work. He has invested a lot of time in showing the property over more than six months, and this is the first offer to come in.

The buyer's broker wants the deal to work as well, believing the property is what the prospective owner is looking for. Both brokers are paid on commission—they get paid only when they sell something. The mortgage broker is also paid on commission. Everyone wants the deal to succeed.

Enter the appraiser—the one person who is intimately involved in real estate transactions who is impartial, and who is duty-bound to find the true value of the property.

"Hit the number"

The vast majority of the time appraisers do their jobs to the best of their ability. They write their reports without interference, concluding that a property is worth a certain amount. But in a growing number of instances, appraisers face pressure to "hit the number." That number is, of course, the selling price of the property. If "the number" that the appraiser arrives at as the value of the property is less than the selling price, the deal may very well fall through.

The pressure can come from the mortgage officer or a broker. It can be subtle, or not so subtle. You might hear something like, "If you have any problems with this property, give me a call." Or, "The loan is for X dollars. If for any reason you are having a tough time getting to that number, give me a call."

John Ross, executive vice president of the Appraisal Institute, says that he has heard complaints from appraisers about this pressure for all of the 15 years that he has been in the industry. But in the past few years, Ross says he has heard more complaints than ever.

The pressure has always been there, but with today's increased property values, the pressure is heightened.

Also, 15 or 20 years ago, property loan products basically consisted of 30-year mortgages that required a significant down payment. Today, property loans that require no money down are available, and many of the refinancing deals that occurred with the record low interest rates from 2001 through 2005 included the owners' taking cash back out of their investment. This has combined to increase risk for lenders. But with these competitive pressures growing, the temptation to cut corners exists.

In a growing real estate market, when loans are made for more than the value of the property, increasing values can often make up the difference in a year or so.

However, should a region's real estate market begin to decline, property owners could be faced with "upside down" mortgages, where the value of the mortgage is higher than that of the property, increasing the risk for lenders that owners will "walk away" from the property. When that happens, the value of the bonds on which the mortgages are backed can lose value, hurting bond investors as well. As you can see, pressure to "hit the number" can affect society as a whole. The job of an appraiser is truly an important one.

Feeling the pressure

Appraisers who feel pressure from mortgage loan originators in banks can file complaints with bank regulators, and appraisers are encouraged to file those complaints. There is no similar official overseer for loan originators of mortgage brokers, according to Ross. He notes that fewer than half of the states regulate mortgage brokers.

How do appraisers avoid the pressure to "hit the number"? Industry experts say that technicians, who provide the most simple forms of appraisals, face pressure more often than analysts who have moved into specialties and who provide more detailed reports at a higher hourly rate.

Appraisers need to make sure they are not reliant on any one client for more than a third of their business, and some experts recommend that the percentage of business from one client be no more than 20 percent. That's because, as the percentage grows, so does the leverage that client has with you. At the same time, you may lose your impartiality if one client is paying a high percentage of your salary.

Honesty, integrity, the only way to do business

With regard to the pressure that appraisers feel to appraise a property at a specific level, John Ross says, "If you are going to be in business a very long time, then you have to do the right thing."

Noting that the pressure on appraisers is greater today than ever before, Ross says that appraisers are put into tough situations every day over the value of properties. "If you are going to stay in the business 5, 10, or 15 years, you cannot afford to succumb to the pressure. Ultimately, if you give in to it, it will come back to haunt you."

Ross urges appraisers to be familiar with their local and state laws so that when they sense pressure they understand how to properly document the situation and how to register complaints with the proper authorities.

George Dell, MAI, SRA, says he was dropped from a lender's approved list of appraisers on several occasions because he resisted coming up with the number that the loan officer needed. "Ninety-nine percent of the time there is no problem or issue," says Dell, adding that the pressure is higher when you are appraising for a refinanced loan and when the economy is weak.

"Some mortgage brokers call appraisers and tell them what the number has to be if they want to get the job," says Anne Johnson MAI, SRA. "That is not acceptable," she says, adding that you can find out pretty quickly whether a client is one that you want to develop a long-term relationship with.

"Bad appraisals drive out good appraisers," says Dell.

Fire clients

Appraisers should spend time networking in their markets, building their reputations, and searching for new business because, just as the appraisal business goes through cycles, so do clients. For a variety of reasons, they may not need your services tomorrow anywhere near as much as they did yesterday.

Another great reason why you should always look for new clients, as well as for more work from your current clients, is that should you feel pressure from one client you have the ability to fire that client without dramatically reducing your income.

Experts say that while firing a client who has been providing you with a significant part of your income is never easy, a week or two after the firing the appraiser is usually quite glad about terminating the relationship. Additionally, working for a client who has a poor reputation can jeopardize your reputation—even if you personally employ the highest standards. As you no doubt have heard many times, it takes a long time to build a quality reputation, but you can lose it in no time at all.

Work hard to protect your reputation. If you bend to pressure to "hit the number" even once, that client will assume you'll do it again and again.

The pressure that appraisers face has even gotten the attention of Congress. The push for legislation that would make it more difficult to get away with applying pressure is growing.

Right from the start, real estate was for him–a conversation with Mark Pomykacz

Growing up in a small town in New Jersey, Mark Pomykacz, MAI, noticed that the richest man in town drove a Rolls Royce, while most of the rest of the residents drove Fords and Chevys. He found out this man was in real estate, and he made up his mind that real estate was the profession for him.

Pomykacz, managing partner of Federal Appraisal & Consulting in Whitehouse Station, N.J., entered the real estate profession right out of college, starting out in sales. Because his income was too sporadic, six months later he looked into real estate appraising, and he has been in the profession ever since.

Challenges to get in

Pomykacz, who has served as president of the New York City Chapter of the Appraisal Institute, often hears the recurring complaint that it is tough to find an appraiser to serve as a trainer and mentor.

Most appraisers who are hiring in his market prefer to hire residential trainees who have some real estate experience. Pomykacz says that employers are very cautious about bringing someone on because it is a multiyear commitment.

As for commercial trainees, he says that those with a banking background traditionally are good candidates, and that a growing number of quality candidates right out of college now have a strong finance or business background.

If he were starting out in the business today, Pomykacz says he would choose commercial appraising because it is a challenging profession that is less crowded and has shorter, shallower business cycles than does the residential side of the business.

Big numbers

Working in the shadow of New York City presents Pomykacz with unique opportunities. "The values are intimidating, and the consequences for mistakes are very dire," he says. For example, teams of appraisers worked on the developing reports following the collapse of the Twin Towers on 9/11.

When dealing with large market valuations, the positives outweigh the negatives, Pomekacz says. Appraisers who serve New York City are very professional, he explains, and because of the size of the market there is ample market data to draw upon (midtown Manhattan has the largest amount of commercial real estate in the country, while lower Manhattan ranks third).

While average residential appraisals in his market range from $300 to $500, Pomykacz's company specializes in investment-grade real estate and special purpose properties such as power plants. The reports for these can be in five volumes of three- to five-inch thick three-ring binders and pay between $25,000 and $125,000.

Pomykacz worked on a team that spent eight weeks appraising Rockefeller Center. He has also appraised a good portion of the Manhattan skyline.

With a staff of 10 appraisers, Pomykacz's company specializes in the market in and around New York City. Most of the company's business comes in via word of mouth, as the company has built a reputation for quality and for getting jobs done on time.

While the company no longer has to spend time and money marketing for new clients, he and his staff do continue to network to maintain the relationships they have developed with lawyers, accountants, property owners, bankers, and mortgage brokers, and that is enough to bring in new clients.

Pomykacz and his staff remain busy as long as the market doesn't stagnate. The 1990s saw a deep real estate recession, worse than the general economy, but the lower interest rates over the past few years have brought the commercial real estate market back, although interest rates have less of an impact on commercial real estate than on residential.

Tomorrow

With more technology on the horizon that will no doubt continue to simplify data gathering for appraisers, Pomykacz says that those entering the profession should be ready to adapt to an increasing reliance on software and other new equipment designed to help do the job more efficiently.

With each piece of commercial real estate posing different challenges for the trainee, it will take about three years for a commercial trainee to become proficient, provided the trainee is partnered with a quality mentor who is skilled in appraising and provides a strong training program, Pomykacz believes.

11

AVMs–how big a threat?

This chapter describes why:

- AVMs have taken business away from residential appraisers.

- Lenders use AVMs primarily to save money.

- Appraisers who have become analysts have seen virtually no impact from AVMs.

Automated Valuation Models (AVMs) have been around for about 20 years. AVMs are basically computer programs that provide a value for a residence.

AVMs are a form of computerized statistical modeling that relies on public records and proprietary databases for information. They are computer programs that use information such as property characteristics, demographics, sales prices, and trends to provide a value externally, removing the human element from the value analysis. Some AVMs allow the user to add or modify information, for example changing square footage, while other AVMs allow no user input.

What AVMs offer is low cost and quick turnaround on appraisal reports. They are often used to provide a value for a refinanced house and for home equity loans, often when the loan-to-value ratio is low. At least seven major AVMs currently exist.

Some appraisers use AVMs in their work. AVMs typically provide valuation only for parts of the country, most commonly in more densely populated areas. Rural areas, which usually don't have online sales database information, are less likely to have AVMs that serve them.

The level of threat to residential appraisers posed by AVMs varies widely depending on whom you speak with. There are those who believe that AVMs spell doom to many residential appraisers. Some say that since the average age of a residential appraiser is approaching 50, when those appraisers retire there will be no need to fill some of those positions with new appraisers because that work will be taken over by AVMs.

Out of the driver's seat

"I personally feel that the client is now in a position to expect to receive what he or she needs," says Bruce Kellogg, MAI. "The appraiser is no longer in a position to tell clients what they need."

In part because of AVMs, appraisers need to serve more as counselors to their clients, partnering with them to ensure their needs are met. Clients won't accept the "one size fits all" mentality of 30 years ago and are now ordering the exact type of report needed— and will continue to do so in the future.

"Time is extremely crucial to clients today," says Dick Powers, 2006 president of the Appraisal Institute, adding that AVMs in some instances provide clients with enough information with which to make lending decisions.

An AVM is simply a way to provide data, says Jack Miller, interviewed in Chapter 3. "If a client wants AVMs, you need to find a way to provide them for him and to keep him happy."

They also point to the fact that during the refinancing boom from 2002 to 2004, lenders were far more likely to use an AVM to value a property, especially when the loan-to-value ratio was low.

Others believe that AVMs pose a dire threat, but only to those who totally focus their energies on the most basic home appraisals. Still others believe that AVMs have been around for 20 years and are likely be around far into the future, but they will pose no bigger threat in 20 years than they do today to the livelihood of residential appraisers.

The issue

"The real issue is, 'What are you getting for your money?' " according to George Dell (see the interview in Chapter 5).

Lenders are pushing for the use of AVMs, says Dell, noting that the pressure on appraisers to complete appraisals better, faster, and cheaper is always there. AVMs can provide appraisals faster and cheaper, but not necessarily better. "Lenders know they need feet on the ground," says Dell.

Of course, AVMs aren't about to disappear, and some enterprising appraisers are finding ways to use and provide AVM information to their clients. Still others are working to develop their own AVMs and/or serving as consultants to AVM manufacturers.

Lenders will need the expertise, as well as the eyes and ears of appraisers, to provide the complete picture of a property. Also, with lenders continuing to offer mortgages with very little down payment, often to those with less-than-perfect credit, the value that an appraiser can bring to the loan approval process only increases.

Most experts agree that to ensure they will continue to earn a good living, residential appraisers should be developing specialties and exploring niches in areas currently untouched by AVMs. Such areas include appraising larger homes, estate valuation, and other types of legal work, to name only a few.

Jeff Grendysa, the only banker on the Appraisal Institute board of directors, says that Appraisal Institute members hold varying opinions about the threat that AVMs pose to the industry, with many feeling they pose a grave threat to the future of residential appraisers. Grendysa, however, believes they don't pose as great a threat as many believe. AVMs do work well for purposes such as portfolio valuations. For example, if an investor needs a $4 billion residential portfolio valued, that investor can't wait a year and a half for all of the individual properties to be valued, nor will the investor be willing to pay for all of the individual appraisers. An AVM fits well in this example.

The bottom line

Every industry is looking for cheaper ways to do things, says Wyoming appraiser Anne Johnson. "We as appraisers need to make better use of AVMs, be the operators, using them as timesavers in our work." Johnson says that the value appraisers bring to their work is their analysis and their eyes and ears. "Machines can't see properties," she says.

Doug Smith, interviewed next, estimates that perhaps 10 percent of residential loans are underwritten using an AVM, and he foresees that proportion increasing, reducing the need for some residential appraisers.

At the same time, Johnson points out some of the AVM shortcomings, noting that AVMs are limited by the information put in and the uniqueness of the property being valued. The AVMs have to be programmed accurately to provide accurate appraisals. As they say, garbage in, garbage out. Whoever feeds in the data needs to know the condition of the property, the economy, and the neighborhood to obtain an accurate valuation. Also, AVMs are unable to identify an overimproved property or other unique attributes of a property that an appraiser would pick up on. Programming and input is critical.

Some appraisers, noting the limited capabilities of existing AVMs, have developed and sold their own AVMs. The key with any AVM is the input of good data. Because of appraisers' local knowledge, they are often in a strong position to develop an AVM for their region.

Grendysa says that what happens on the residential side of the business is often followed years later on the commercial side. For example, the multiple listing service (MLS) data providers of sales information first began providing information to residential appraisers, so you are likely to see an increase in data sources available for commercial appraisals in the future. Can AVMs for commercial properties be far behind?

Some appraisers today are providing AVM-generated reports to their clients, while still others are working on their own forms of AVMs or are serving as consultants to companies that are developing new, more sophisticated AVMs.

Although it is impossible to tell how quickly the use of AVMs will increase, experts all agree that appraisers must be aware of the AVM products in the market and understand their strengths and weaknesses.

Find a niche–a conversation with Doug Smith

Most real estate appraisers begin as residential appraisers. Then some move on to become commercial appraisers. Doug Smith did things differently: he used his 32 years of experience in the hotel industry to help several Montana commercial appraisers to complete reports.

Then he decided to enter the appraising business for himself. Later he partnered with a residential appraiser who taught him that part of the business.

Smith developed a specialty in repossessed properties, and now he has a built a substantial business in repossessed properties in southwest Montana. "No one wants to deal with them," he says about repossessed properties, adding that working on the reports for them is sometimes dangerous, and there can be a lot of detail work when estimating necessary repairs.

Trainee advice

Smith recommends that trainees follow the Appraisal Institute education track "and not mess around with others." Smith says that appraisers can "stand out from the clutter by having the very best in education," and he further encourages appraisers to continue on to get their SRA or MAI from the Appraisal Institute, adding that both designations can be completed by working diligently for four to six years.

Appraisers who continue their educations and develop specialties can continue to do $300 to $500 reports, but are also qualified to appraise the $3 to $5 million property for $2,500.

"It is just a matter of arithmetic," says Smith. "How many reports can you do and how much can you charge over a period of time?"

"You need to be learning something all the time," says Smith, adding that appraisers should be subscribing to forums and reading magazines and books targeted to their profession. "Stay fresh and educate yourself," he says.

Stay out of the trap

Too often appraisers fall into the trap of working harder and harder, believing that if they aren't working they are not making money, which Smith warns is short-sighted. Working too many hours often leads to a reduction in productivity, so appraisers need to balance work and take time off to recharge themselves.

For example, Smith organized his work so he was able to take four weeks of vacation in 2005, making sure that he had plenty of time to relax and recharge his batteries. New appraisers might not be able to afford to take that much time off, but he believes it's important to take some time for yourself to avoid job burnout.

Smith says that appraisers need to allocate time to prospect for new clients, spending time every week with lenders, professionals such as lawyers and accountants, and relocation organizations. Appraisers also need to spend time with current clients to ensure their current and future appraisal needs are being met.

Smith sees a continuation of technology enhancements that will make it easier for appraisers to turn out high-quality reports quickly. For example, he spent $600 on a laser measuring device that cuts 20 minutes off the time needed to measure homes. "I can stay in one place and with two clicks have the size of the room," he says.

Smith remembers that he formerly had boxes of flood maps in his office. When a property was in a flood zone, he had to go through the box, find the correct map, then scan it into the report. Today, Smith has a software program that includes the flood maps that he needs, allowing him to quickly download any portion of a map into his report.

Software also quickly and easily provides comparable details, such as the distance to the property being appraised, eliminating the need to develop the detailed information by hand.

"Appraisers who embrace technology will put more money in their pockets on a daily basis by effectively using enhanced tools to more quickly complete tasks," says Smith.

Coming back for more

What keeps Smith, who is in his 60s, enthusiastic about real estate appraising? Every assignment is different.

For example, Smith was asked by a couple to appraise a manufactured home on leased property, something that he hadn't done before. He also determined the value of a mining claim.

Smith urges new appraisers not to give in to pressure to "hit the number" that some lenders apply. Build your reputation on having the highest ethics, and you build your business for the long run.

12

Staying in or getting out

This chapter describes:

- Ten keys to avoiding burnout
- Why you don't have to retire

One thing that attracts candidates to the real estate appraising profession is the opportunity to continue working well past normal retirement age. Although there can be some physical demands to the job, appraisers normally gain knowledge and skill every year they are in the business so that an appraiser with 20 years of experience should be able to complete a higher quality appraisal in less time than someone with only five years of experience. Most have stopped being technicians years ago and are now valued analysts.

Veteran appraisers have the experience of being efficient schedulers—combining similar tasks to improve efficiency. Selecting proper comparables, which can be the most difficult part of the job to learn for many appraisers, becomes easier with experience; appraisers have a bank of appraising knowledge from which to draw to quickly identify quality comparables.

Yet appraisers do face job burnout. For appraisers who have chosen to work on their own or for an appraisal firm as an independent contractor, it is too easy to fall into the trap of doing "just one more appraisal."

Because most appraisers are paid like salespeople in that the more they "sell" the higher their pay, the temptation to do "just one more" appraisal, which then leads to another, is difficult to overcome. Few people will tell you they couldn't use a few more dollars in their paycheck, and appraisers are no different.

But continuing to do more appraisals and extending the day ever longer often leads to a difficult home life and to job burnout.

Pressures

Appraisers have difficult jobs. You often feel pressure from a lender to "hit the number." There is ever-changing technology to keep up with. You have continuing education requirements to maintain your license. You may choose to continue your education and pursue a professional designation. Marketing your business is a never-ending process. Getting involved with professional organizations can help jump start an appraisal business, or put it into high gear.

And then there are the pressures from home—college educations to fund, weddings to pay for, the mortgage on your primary residence. What about that vacation home you have your eye on? And don't forget about funding your eventual retirement.

Completing another appraisal isn't an issue, so long as you do so because you have increased your efficiency and aren't taking more time away from your family, or sacrificing the little bit of relaxation that can help you to recharge your batteries. The problem occurs when the end of the day goes from 5:00 to 6:00 and then to 7:00 on a regular basis.

There are always crunch times during which you will need to put in extra hours to complete an appraisal you have promised a client. But when the 40-hour weeks regularly turn to 50, 60, then 70 hours, you are headed toward burning out: being less productive on the job, and not very pleasant to be around at home.

Here are 10 keys to avoiding burning out.

1. *Do what you love.* If you are continuing to do the same type of appraisals that you were doing 5 or 10 years ago and find yourself stuck in a rut and bored, it is time to start in a new direction. Appraisers who find the right niche for themselves are happier, enjoy what they do, realize that they provide a valuable service to society, are professionally challenged, and often give back to their profession to make it better. Appraisers who have carved out their own niches find themselves working for and with people they like. They enjoy going to the office and don't mind putting in the extra effort. Those appraisers who don't like their jobs, but are unwilling to spend the time networking to find niches that excite them, can find themselves burning out. They find it difficult to get up in the morning. They are less than enthusiastic toward their work, which can result in having less work to do. Their home life is likely suffering as well. Spend the time necessary to find the niche that excites and challenges you and go for it. And then don't become complacent—in a year or two you may need new challenges. After you are licensed and have a couple of years of experience under your belt, make sure you are doing a job that interests and challenges you. Strive to be a valued analyst like other leaders in the industry.

2. *Don't continue to do things you have always done in the way you have always done them.* Working the same routine every day will ensure that your job will get monotonous. Look at your work the way an outsider might. Examine the many different facets of your daily job and look for new and better ways in which to do them. Develop routines that improve efficiency. But becoming complacent and assuming your way is the only way to get the job done can lead you into a rut that slowly saps your energy and ability to think in new and exciting ways. Continually look for ways to improve your efficiency, especially when completing administrative tasks, so that you spend most of your energy doing the parts of the job that most interest you. The better you are able to

reduce the part of the day spent on mundane tasks, the more time you will have to pursue the parts of the profession that attracted you to it in the first place.

3. *Reach out to your peers and learn their best practices and adapt them to your style.* Look at how both veterans and rookies are tackling their jobs. Visit an appraiser you would like to emulate in his or her office to see how he or she does the job. This suggestion goes for those new to the profession as well as those with 10 or 20 years of experience. For the newcomer, it is essential at first to follow the procedures set down by your mentor. But after licensing, you may want to branch out and talk with other top appraisers to learn how they efficiently complete their jobs. For the more experienced appraiser who may be looking to develop a new niche, finding others who already serve that niche can shorten the learning cycle and help the appraiser to begin in the market like a veteran, rather than a newcomer, which should lead to higher efficiency and a higher per-hour rate. And for the veteran, there are your peers who may be at higher levels of the business. It may require getting on a plane and flying across the country, but your visit can reap rewards many times over. And don't overlook the new recruit who is a technology wizard. He or she may point you to much higher productivity simply by taking advantage of the latest technology rather than muddling through trying to research and learn on your own.

4. *Network with your peers.* The two previous examples show the importance of networking with your peers. On top of learning how to complete the technical parts of your job, you need to remain active in your profession so that you can respond to changes in your industry. The key is to see a trend coming and to develop a response to it. Reacting to a marketplace change after it has occurred isn't the way to succeed. Network with your peers by becoming active on at least the local level. Also consider becoming active on the state and then national levels to expose yourself to broader coming trends. The value of real estate transactions is increasing at a rapid pace, meaning that the importance of receiving accurate valuations will become more of a policy issue for state and national

lawmakers. You will need to keep up on legislative changes because they will increasingly impact your job going forward.

5. *Network with professionals with whom you work.* Networking with your peers is critical, but spending time networking with professionals, such as loan officers, real estate brokers, attorneys, and accountants, is also something you need to fit into your workweek. To get an accurate representation of where the appraisal industry is and where it may be heading, you need the perspective of professionals both within the industry and those who support it. While you are networking with these professionals, you will also be building your reputation and perhaps finding a niche that provides you with a growing, challenging opportunity. Appraisers often analyze the market and determine which parts of it are underserved. But appraisers are as likely to find that underserved part of the market simply by networking with professionals, spending time asking good questions, and listening much more than talking.

6. *Consider earning an industry designation.* Many appraisers in more populated areas understand the value of receiving an industry designation. It provides them with tools to do their jobs better. It also shows the market they serve that they take their profession seriously enough to spend time to qualify for and retain a designation that many other appraisers don't bother to earn. In competitive markets, appraisers with designations looking to carve out their own niches can find more success than those without designations. And as the market becomes more global every day, designations will continue to grow in value in all markets.

7. *Make technology your friend.* If you are an early adopter of technology, find yourself enjoying the challenge of the newest software programs, have mastered the use of online databases, great. Keep up the good work. Those appraisers who embrace technology have seen their hourly rate improve as the cost per appraisal remains fairly flat. If technology isn't one of your strong points, then befriend someone who embraces it. Technology will continue to shape the future of appraising. The mantra of appraising today is "better, faster, cheaper." The best way to get better, faster, and cheaper long term is through better use of technology. Yes, you

can improve how you complete administrative tasks. And yes, as you grow as a professional appraiser you should be able to complete jobs quicker. And you can get more done by working longer hours in the short term, but that doesn't work very well over the long term. The proper use of technology—which doesn't mean using every new program or device out there, but instead selecting those pieces of technology that improve your efficiency—will result in your being able to deliver better, faster, and cheaper reports. That mantra is here today and shows no signs of changing. Long term, technology can help you improve your efficiency to keep your income on the rise.

8. *Get fit.* Study after study shows that people who exercise not only have more energy and feel better physically, but their mental outlook on today and tomorrow improves. People who spend a half hour or more exercising daily find they have more physical and mental energy with which to tackle their day. People who exercise are generally more pleased with their physical appearance, which improves the way in which they carry themselves. There is no reason why appraisers in their 50s can't get themselves into better shape than they were in 20 years ago.

9. *Eat properly.* Eating properly can be a challenge for appraisers who are facing tight deadlines and the daily "better, faster, cheaper" mantra. But ensuring that you are eating healthy food, rather than a daily dose of donuts and fries, will improve how you view yourself and your energy level. Dozens of diets offer many different types of advice. Find one that works for you, and then modify your food intake on a permanent basis to keep with the overall focus of the plan. You can't stay "on a diet" for the rest of your life, but you can follow a diet's overall guidelines on a permanent basis. To get started, try this: watch your portions; dramatically reduce your intake of food with high-sugar content; cut out white bread and replace it with whole wheat; dramatically reduce fatty foods and starches; eat five smaller meals a day rather than three large ones. The next time you go to the doctor take a look at how much you weighed 10 to 15 years ago and make that weight your goal.

10. *Strive for work/life balance.* This will be a challenge your entire career. As a new recruit, you will have to put in long hours to learn the business and to show your mentor you are serious about becoming a first-class professional. As you move further into your career, you may look to strike out on your own, to carve your own niche, to make more money to support your family. It is important professionally to strive for new heights. But at the same time you need to make sure you aren't ignoring your significant other and your children. Avoiding job burnout often includes making sure you take vacations. You might have to take short vacations at first as you are getting started and just developing a reputation. But even as a sole proprietor you should be able to take longer vacations as the years go by, perhaps developing a strategic alliance with a peer, so that your customers receive the same high-level service when you are away as when you are on the job. You've heard it before—nobody goes to their grave saying they wish they had finished just one more appraisal. Work hard to provide the standard of living that you and your family have chosen, but make sure you don't lose the things that money can't buy, like close personal relationships with those you love. Appraisers at the top of their profession who also have strong family relationships have learned how to balance work with family time. Just make sure while you are climbing the ladder that you aren't losing touch with the reason you want to climb that ladder, or the support on which your ladder rests.

Planning to retire?

The appraisal profession is one that employs many part-time appraisers, many of whom are semi-retired. For those who find it daunting to save enough to actually retire on a full-time basis, the profession offers the opportunity to supplement your income without making a full-time commitment.

Appraisers can often find plenty of part-time work in the location in which they want to retire because popular retirement destinations (the

Carolinas, Florida, Cape Cod, Las Vegas, etc.) often have booming seasonal real estate markets—with substantial numbers of appraisals that need to be done. Popular retirement locations may offer work on a seasonal basis that won't support an entire full-time staff.

Other appraisers choose not to work part-time, but rather to retire from the business. When asked if she plans to retire, Wyoming appraiser Anne Johnson provides a quick, one-word answer: "Yes!"

If you plan to retire and sell your appraisal business, the key is to make sure you have something to sell. As your career progresses, you should be building your business and perhaps adding a staff of appraisers, one of whom may be interested in eventually buying it from you. You should also be growing your client base and developing specialties to better serve your market.

Basing your business on just a handful of clients is dangerous in the short run. In the long run, it can make your business much less valuable to someone who may be thinking about buying it.

When building your business you will probably look to diversify to help smooth out the deep cycles that can greatly decrease the amount of work you have. An outsider who is considering purchasing your business will be looking for the same thing—how steady is the stream of income and how prone is it to deep business cycles? A business that is based on established clients, some of which pay higher than average rates for more detailed and specialized reports, will be worth more than one based on the most basic of appraisals.

Because a majority of appraisers operate as sole proprietors, and those who don't often work in small companies with fewer than 10 employees, finding someone to purchase your business often means a peer or employee who has worked with you.

Getting top dollar for a business often means that the new owner is on staff for a minimum of six months to a year prior (sometimes much longer) to ensure a smooth handoff so that customers know the person who is buying the firm and are confident that he or she will continue to provide the same or a higher level of service. Sometimes the owner agrees to stay on a part-time basis for continuity and stability, not to mention a continuing stream of income.

Making the balancing act work–a conversation with Jeff Grendysa

As a mortgage banker with a southeast Michigan-based bank, Jeff Grendysa, SRA, works a balancing act as he decides which appraisers to contract with. Grendysa says that bankers today are looking for a fast, good report but, like any other professionals, they are under pressure to keep costs down.

While Grendysa won't trade price for quality, price remains an important consideration. Grendysa and other bankers do their best to match the detail of the report needed with the background of the appraiser they hire, understanding that they will pay more for a more detailed report.

For example, if a loan is requested for a house in a subdivision where the bank provided a loan for a similar house across the street last year, the market has remained fairly stable, and the credit of the person requesting the loan is strong, chances are the banker won't need a more detailed report.

On the other hand, should a loan be requested for a multimillion-dollar new house in an area of large, new homes, the loan officer will likely look to a residential appraiser who is skilled in large home appraisals and can provide a quality detailed report, drawing in comparables that help show the home's value clearly.

"It takes a long time for an appraiser to build a strong reputation," says Grendysa, "but a reputation can be ruined quickly, as news travels fast. Bankers do realize that everyone is human, and they don't always remove an appraiser from their approved list should the appraiser make a mistake. But at the same time it is no different than other professions. If the mistake costs the client money, you'll likely not be invited back again," he says.

Good reports, bad reports

Grendysa says that loan officers are always looking for a good report that is characterized by the data being presented in such a way that it is easy to see how all of the information fits together, leading you to a logical conclusion about the value of the real estate. If the reader can't follow the information contained in the report, has a difficult time reaching the same conclusion, or information is missing, the report becomes suspect, and the appraiser will probably not get as much work from that institution going forward.

The two most common trainee shortcomings are a lack of technical skills and still undeveloped judgmental skills. It would be easy for a trainee to misjudge comparable sales, put them into a report, analyze them, draw conclusions, and arrive at a value that is unreliable.

It comes down to developing good judgment through experience, practice, and good direction from someone you work with, comments Grendysa, who says he was fortunate to study with a mentor who instilled the importance of writing good narratives, of being inquisitive, and of solving problems, all of which help lead to quality reports.

Getting started

Studying real estate at Eastern Michigan University, Grendysa saw the hot real estate market of the 1980s and was attracted to the profession. Students in many of his college real estate classes were interested in becoming real estate appraisers at the time.

Grendysa says that when he graduated, he had enough presence not to chase a high income "right out of the gate." Instead he chose long-term opportunity and quality training. He was introduced to Roger Everett, who was in charge of the appraisal department at Manufacturers Hanover Mortgage Corporation. Everett, who became Grendysa's mentor, chaired the education committee for the Society of Real Estate Appraisers, one of the organizations that later merged to become the Appraisal Institute.

While at Manufacturers Hanover, where he stayed for 18 years, Grendysa not only worked on appraisals, but also ran the underwriting department and then moved on to branch administration. After the company's acquisition, he became head of retail operations. He left that job, going back to appraisals, until he was contacted by the president of the bank for which he now works.

Developing a partnership

Because he has worked both as a banker and an appraiser, Grendysa clearly understands the partnership that must develop between the loan officer and the appraiser in order to create a quality report. Grendysa says that a harmonious relationship requires that both the appraiser and loan officer clearly communicate expectations, so that the appraiser can develop a report that fulfills the loan officer's requirements.

For example, Grendysa says that for a commercial assignment, he might be considering lending in a geographic area where the market and current economic conditions are uncertain. The property might be priced at $150 per square foot for new construction, but he would need an appraiser's opinion regarding the supply and demand for similar commercial space in order to conduct an analysis and draw a conclusion as to whether the property was worth the negotiated price.

Appraisers must also be in tune with highest and best uses of a property. Grendysa recently worked on a potential loan for a residential property that was located in an industrial zone. The appraiser had to look deeply to determine the highest and best use, which in this case was residential because the surrounding property was not suited to industrial uses.

PART FIVE

Appendixes

Appendix 1
Who sets
the rules?

The Appraisal Foundation, through its Appraisal Standards Board, publishes the *Uniform Standards of Professional Appraisal Practice* (USPAP), the generally accepted set of performance standards for residential and commercial appraisers. These standards are enforced by states and by various professional appraisal organizations. In addition, the minimum qualifications for real estate appraisers (as well as other types of appraisers) are established by the Appraiser Qualifications Board (AQB) of The Appraisal Foundation.

When entering the profession, trainees follow rules as outlined by the AQB. The AQB develops the minimum federal standards that each state must follow to certify residential and general (also known as commercial) appraisers.

States must abide by these minimum guidelines, and some have chosen to make their requirements more stringent than the federal standards.

The AQB also mandates that to renew an appraisal license, every two years licensed appraisers must complete a seven-hour national course (some states require the course every year).

USPAP

Trainees are made aware of USPAP standards early in their careers because trainees in all states are required to take a 15-hour course (or an equivalent) that helps them to understand their industry's guiding principles.

The USPAP course touches on all real estate appraisal standards, and it also provides advisory opinions and additional guidance from the USPAP standards board. There are 10 standards in all: two focus on real property appraising; another covers review appraisals (appraisals that are done to review work already done by a licensed appraiser); and others cover different types of appraisals, including real property, personal property, and business valuation.

The course covers topics such as:

- History of USPAP
- Professionalism
- Valuation services and appraisal practice
- Ethics Rule
- Competency Rule
- Departure Rule
- Supplemental Standards Rule
- Discounted cash-flow analysis
- Retrospective value opinions
- Prospective value opinions
- Identifying the client's intended use to develop a report
- Use of an Automated Valuation Model (AVM)
- Business appraisal and development
- Business appraisal and reporting

Focusing on the requirements for ethical behavior and competent performance by appraisers, the course was developed in 1998 and is revised annually for The Appraisal Foundation with assistance from the Education Council of Appraisal Foundation Sponsors. Emphasizing the role of the appraiser and the impartiality associated with the profession, the course also outlines the special responsibilities of the appraiser as an impartial party in a real estate transaction.

Guiding principles

Both residential and commercial appraisers refer to USPAP as guiding principles for the appraisal profession. Both the 7- and 15-hour courses must be taught by instructors certified by The Appraisal Foundation. Those instructors must be in good standing with The Appraisal Foundation, meet teaching and appraisal experience standards, attend a course, and pass a rigorous exam at the completion of the course.

John Brenan, director of Research and Technical Issues for The Appraisal Foundation, says that the bottom line is if someone performs ethically by the Ethics Rule, and competently in accordance with the Competency Rule, then "everything would fall into place." Brenan says that most appraisers have a set practice, performing the same type of appraisals on a weekly and monthly basis, and when working within their specialties have little need to go back to the two rules.

When appraisers branch out and perform appraisals that are not what they typically do, they would be more likely to refer to USPAP. For example, Brenan says that an appraiser who may specialize in office buildings might receive a call to complete an appraisal on a dairy farm. If that appraiser can't work with another appraiser who has expertise in dairy farm appraisals, or can't get the education he or she feels necessary to complete a quality report, the appraiser, consulting the USPAP Competency Rule, would have to turn down the assignment.

Under the Competency Rule, prior to accepting an assignment, the appraiser must properly identify the job that needs to be done and have the knowledge and expertise to complete the assignment or, alternatively, he or she must:

1. Disclose the lack of knowledge and/or expertise to the client before accepting the assignment
2. Take all steps necessary or appropriate to complete the assignment competently
3. Describe the lack of knowledge and/or expertise and the steps taken to competently complete the assignment in the report

Another example would be an appraiser who gets a call from a relative who is a mortgage banker and wants to use the appraiser's services.

That appraiser would go back to the Ethics Rule to determine under what conditions he could accept assignments from a relative.

The Ethics Rule is comprised of four sections:

1. *Conduct.* This section of the Ethics Rule states that an appraiser must perform assignments ethically and competently, in accordance with USPAP and any supplemental standards agreed to by the appraiser in accepting the assignment. An appraiser must not engage in criminal conduct. An appraiser must perform assignments with impartiality, objectivity, and independence, and without accommodation of personal interests.
2. *Management.* This section states that the payment of undisclosed fees, commissions, or things of value in connection with the procurement of an assignment is unethical.
3. *Confidentiality.* This part of the rule states that an appraiser must protect the confidential nature of the appraiser–client relationship. An appraiser must act in good faith with regard to the legitimate interests of the client in the use of confidential information and in the communication of assignment results.
4. *Record keeping.* This part of the Ethics Rule states that the appraiser must prepare a work file for each appraisal that includes the name of the client and the identity, by name or type, of any other intended users; true copies of any written reports, documented on any type of media; summaries of any oral reports or testimony, or a transcript of testimony, including the appraiser's signed and dated certification; and all other data, information, and documentation necessary to support the appraiser's opinions and conclusions.

First promulgated in 1987, USPAP has received criticism from some appraisers that the rules do change too frequently (annually), making it challenging for appraisers to keep up with the most current standards. Brennan says that over the years the standards have been adjusted and enhanced.

Sweeping 2006 change

A June 2006 update is the most sweeping in at least 10 years, removing the Departure Rule from USPAP.

In July 1994, the Departure Rule was added to USPAP to clarify the difference between limited versus complete appraisals, but since then it has created more confusion than clarity in the marketplace. Brennan says that the public often assumes that complete appraisals are better than limited appraisals and are preferred in all circumstances.

He explains that limited appraisals aren't always less reliable or less viable than complete appraisals. A complete appraisal is one that has utilized all three appraisal approaches:

- Cost
- Sales comparison
- Income

Nothing in the standards specifies the level of inspection that an appraiser must do to comply with the standards, says Brennan. This leads to confusion, as appraisers receive no guidance as to whether they need to go inside the property or simply drive by to be in compliance.

Here is an example of not needing a full appraisal to provide a complete report. You could perform a full inspection of a residential property in a newer subdivision and have at your fingertips an abundance of information about homes sold during the past three months that are the same as the property being appraised. In this example, the income approach might not be applicable as the proposed buyer would occupy the residence.

If you only completed a sales comparison approach, that would be considered a limited appraisal. However, you may have physically inspected the property, going inside the home. Using the recent sales history you could put together a report that may be more reliable to a lender than would a complete appraisal. Because the Departure Rule does not specify the level of inspection, a complete appraisal on this property could be developed by an appraiser who never inspected the property and has little information about the physical condition of the home.

Scope of Work Rule

The 2006 change removing the Departure Rule replaces it with the Scope of Work Rule. Under this new rule, appraisers need to develop a scope of work that will produce credible work, removing the limited or complete report terminology from USPAP.

The goal of the 2006 change is to help the appraiser better understand that USPAP provides flexibility and information about how to handle assignments within generally accepted standards. Although appraisers have complained that USPAP is too broad and vague, Brennan says that the standards are written to provide flexibility to complete assignments ethically and competently without dictating specific methodology and technique.

The Scope of Work rule will change the way appraisers work on reports, from top down (following prescribed guidelines for developing reports) to bottom up (examining what work needs to be done to develop a credible report). This rule will change the way appraisers develop their plan of work, no longer relying on the USPAP to dictate the work that needs to be done, shifting the burden to the appraiser to use the tools necessary to develop credible reports.

Appraisers on some assignments may need to go back to their clients and explain that their scope of work is incomplete. They will need to provide clients with a rationale for why additional work needs to be done. As a result, the client will either need to accept the additional work and cost associated with it or face the potential of receiving a less than complete report. Therefore, the onus will shift to the appraiser to be certain that the scope of work is complete.

Keeping up

A key to remaining current in the industry is keeping up to date on the latest changes to USPAP. The Appraisal Foundation posts USPAP updates on its Web site and, on a monthly basis, adds to its site's frequently asked questions section, keeping appraisers up to date with the most current guidance.

Additionally, those appraisers who don't frequent the Web site may also choose to take advantage of subscription services that provide detailed information on USPAP. Going forward, annual changes will be replaced with an 18-month update, then a two-year update beginning in 2008.

Who sets the rules?

Portions of The Uniform Standards of Professional Appraisal Practice (USPAP) copyright © 2005 by The Appraisal Foundation are reproduced with permission of The Appraisal Foundation.

The Competency Rule and the Ethics Rule are a reproduction of *only a portion* of the 2005 Edition, and complete copies of USPAP (including Advisory Opinions and Statements) are available for purchase from The Appraisal Foundation, 1029 Vermont Avenue, NW, Suite 900, Washington D.C., 2005.

Appendix 2

Competency Rule

Prior to accepting an assignment or entering into an agreement to perform any assignment, an appraiser must properly identify the problem to be addressed and have the knowledge and experience to complete the assignment competently. Alternatively, an appraiser must do the following:

1. Disclose the lack of knowledge and/or experience to the client before accepting the assignment,
2. Take all steps necessary or appropriate to complete the assignment competently, and
3. Describe the lack of knowledge and/or experience and the steps taken to complete the assignment competently in the report.

Comment: Competency applies to factors such as, but not limited to, an appraiser's familiarity with a specific type of property, a market, a geographic area, or an analytical method. If such a factor is necessary for an appraiser to develop credible assignment results, the appraiser is responsible for having the competency to address that factor or for following the steps outlined above to satisfy this Competency Rule.

The background and experience of appraisers varies widely, and a lack of knowledge or experience can lead to inaccurate or inappropriate appraisal practice. The Competency Rule requires an appraiser to have both the knowledge and the experience required to perform a specific appraisal service competently.

If an appraiser is offered the opportunity to perform an appraisal service but lacks the necessary knowledge or experience to complete it competently, the appraiser must disclose his or her lack of knowledge or experience to the client before accepting the assignment and then take the necessary or appropriate steps to complete the appraisal service competently. This may be accomplished in various ways, including, but not limited to, personal study by the appraiser, association with an appraiser reasonably believed to have the necessary knowledge or experience, or retention of others who possess the required knowledge or experience.

In an assignment where geographic competency is necessary, an appraiser preparing an appraisal in an unfamiliar location must spend sufficient time to understand the nuances of the local market and the supply and demand factors relating to the specific property type and the location involved. Such understanding will not be imparted solely from a consideration of specific data such as demographics, costs, sales, and rentals. The necessary understanding of local market conditions provides the bridge between a sale and a comparable sale or a rental and a comparable rental. If an appraiser is not in a position to spend the necessary amount of time in a market area to obtain this understanding, affiliation with a qualified local appraiser may be the appropriate response to ensure development of credible assignment results.

Although this rule requires an appraiser to identify the problem and disclose any deficiency in competence prior to accepting an assignment, facts or conditions uncovered during the course of an assignment could cause an appraiser to discover that he or she lacks the required knowledge or experience to complete the assignment competently. At the point of such discovery, the appraiser is obligated to notify the client and comply with items 2 and 3 of this rule.

Competency Rule

The Competency Rule is a reproduction of *only a portion* of the 2005 Edition, and complete copies of USPAP (including Advisory Opinions and Statements) are available for purchase from The Appraisal Foundation, 1029 Vermont Avenue, NW, Suite 900, Washington, D.C. 20005.

Appendix 3

Ethics Rule

To promote and preserve the public trust inherent in professional appraisal practice, an appraiser must observe the highest standards of professional ethics. This Ethics Rule is divided into four sections: Conduct, Management, Confidentiality, and Record Keeping. The first three sections apply to all appraisal practice, and all four sections apply to appraisal practice performed under Standards 1 through 10.

Comment: This Rule specifies the personal obligations and responsibilities of the individual appraiser. However, it should also be noted that groups and organizations engaged in appraisal practice share the same ethical obligations.

Compliance with USPAP is required when either the service or the appraiser is obligated by law or regulation, or by agreement with the client or intended users, to comply. In addition to these requirements, an individual should comply any time that individual represents that he or she is performing the service as an appraiser.

An appraiser must not misrepresent his or her role when providing valuation services that are outside of appraisal practice.

Comment: Honesty, impartiality, and professional competency are required of all appraisers under these *Uniform Standards of Professional Appraisal Practice* (USPAP). To document recognition and acceptance of his or her USPAP-related responsibilities in communicating an appraisal, appraisal review, or appraisal consulting assignment completed under USPAP, an appraiser is required to certify compliance with USPAP.

Conduct

An appraiser must perform assignments ethically and competently, in accordance with USPAP and any supplemental standards agreed to by the appraiser in accepting the assignment. An appraiser must not engage in criminal conduct. An appraiser must perform assignments with impartiality, objectivity, and independence, and without accommodation of personal interests.

In appraisal practice, an appraiser must not perform as an advocate for any party or issue.

Comment: An appraiser may be an advocate only in support of his or her assignment results. Advocacy in any other form in appraisal practice is a violation of the Ethics Rule.

An appraiser must not accept an assignment that includes the reporting of predetermined opinions and conclusions.

An appraiser must not communicate assignment results in a misleading or fraudulent manner. An appraiser must not use or communicate a misleading or fraudulent report or knowingly permit an employee or other person to communicate a misleading or fraudulent report.

An appraiser must not use or rely on unsupported conclusions relating to characteristics such as race, color, religion, national origin, gender, marital status, familial status, age, receipt of public assistance income, handicap, or an unsupported conclusion that homogeneity of such characteristics is necessary to maximize value.

Comment: An individual appraiser employed by a group or organization that conducts itself in a manner that does not conform to these standards should take steps that are appropriate under the circumstances to ensure compliance with the standards.

Management

The payment of undisclosed fees, commissions, or things of value in connection with the procurement of an assignment is unethical.

Comment: Disclosure of fees, commissions, or things of value connected to the procurement of an assignment must appear in the certification and in any transmittal letter in which conclusions are stated. In groups or organizations engaged in appraisal practice, intracompany payments to employees for business development are not considered to be unethical. Competency, rather than financial incentives, should be the primary basis for awarding an assignment.

It is unethical for an appraiser to accept an assignment, or to have a compensation arrangement for an assignment, that is contingent on any of the following:

1. The reporting of a predetermined result (e.g., opinion of value),
2. A direction in assignment results that favors the cause of the client,
3. The amount of a value opinion,
4. The attainment of a stipulated result, or
5. The occurrence of a subsequent event directly related to the appraiser's opinions and specific to the assignment's purpose.

Advertising for or soliciting assignments in a manner that is false, misleading, or exaggerated is unethical.

Comment: In groups or organizations engaged in appraisal practice, decisions concerning finder or referral fees, contingent compensation, and advertising may not be the responsibility of an individual appraiser, but for a particular assignment, it is the responsibility of the individual appraiser to ascertain that there has been no breach of ethics, that the assignment is prepared in accordance with these Standards, and that the report can be properly certified when required by Standards Rules 2-3, 3-3, 5-3, 6-8, 8-3, or 10-3.

Confidentiality

An appraiser must protect the confidential nature of the appraiser–client relationship.

An appraiser must act in good faith with regard to the legitimate interests of the client in the use of confidential information and in the communication of assignment results.

An appraiser must be aware of, and comply with, all confidentiality and privacy laws and regulations applicable in an assignment.*

An appraiser must not disclose confidential information or assignment results prepared for a client to anyone other than the client and persons specifically authorized by the client, state enforcement agencies and such third parties as may be authorized by due process of law, and a duly authorized professional peer review committee except when such disclosure to a committee would violate applicable law or regulation. It is unethical for a member of a duly authorized professional peer review committee to disclose confidential information presented to the committee.

Comment: When all confidential elements of confidential information are removed through redaction or the process of aggregation, client authorization is not required for the disclosure of the remaining information, as modified.

Record keeping

An appraiser must prepare a workfile for each appraisal, appraisal review, or appraisal consulting assignment. The workfile must include:

- The name of the client and the identity, by name or type, of any other intended users,
- True copies of any written reports, documented on any type of media,
- Summaries of any oral reports or testimony, or a transcript of testimony, including the appraiser's signed and dated certification, and
- All other data, information, and documentation necessary to support the appraiser's opinions and conclusions and to show compliance

*NOTICE: Pursuant to the passage of the Gramm-Leach-Bliley Act in 1999, numerous agencies have adopted new privacy regulations. Such regulations are focused on the protection of information provided by consumers to those involved in financial activities "found to be closely related to banking or usual in connection with the transaction of banking." These activities have been deemed to include "appraising real or personal property." (Quotations are from the Federal Trade Commission, Privacy of Consumer Financial Information; Final Rule, 16 CFR Part 313.)

with this Rule and all other applicable Standards, or references to the location(s) of such other documentation.

An appraiser must retain the workfile for a period of at least five years after preparation or at least two years after final disposition of any judicial proceeding in which the appraiser provided testimony related to the assignment, whichever period expires last.

An appraiser must have custody of his or her workfile, or make appropriate workfile retention, access, and retrieval arrangements with the party having custody of the workfile.

Comment: A workfile preserves evidence of the appraiser's consideration of all applicable data and statements required by USPAP and other information as may be required to support the appraiser's opinions, conclusions, and recommendations. For example, the content of a workfile for a Complete Appraisal must reflect consideration of all USPAP requirements applicable to the specific Complete Appraisal assignment. However, the content of a workfile for a Limited Appraisal need only reflect consideration of the USPAP requirements from which there have been no departure and that are required by the specific Limited Appraisal assignment.

A photocopy or an electronic copy of the entire actual written appraisal, appraisal review, or appraisal consulting report sent or delivered to a client satisfies the requirement of a true copy. As an example, a photocopy or electronic copy of the Self-Contained Appraisal Report, Summary Appraisal Report, or Restricted Use Appraisal Report actually issued by an appraiser for a real property appraisal assignment satisfies the true copy requirement for that assignment.

Care should be exercised in the selection of the form, style, and type of medium for written records, which may be handwritten and informal, to ensure that they are retrievable by the appraiser throughout the prescribed record retention period.

A workfile must be in existence prior to and contemporaneous with the issuance of a written or oral report. A written summary of an oral report must be added to the workfile within a reasonable time after the issuance of the oral report.

A workfile must be made available by the appraiser when required by state enforcement agencies or due process of law. In addition, a workfile in support of a Restricted Use Appraisal Report must be sufficient for the appraiser to produce a Summary Appraisal Report (for assignments under Standards 2 and 8) or an Appraisal Report (for assignments under Standard 10), and must be available for inspection by the client in accordance with the Comment to Standards Rules 2-2(c)(ix), 8-2(c)(ix), and 10-2(b)(ix).

The Ethics Rule is a reproduction of *only a portion* of the 2005 Edition, and complete copies of USPAP (including Advisory Opinions and Statements) are available for purchase from The Appraisal Foundation, 1029Vermont Avenue, NW, Suite 900, Washington, D.C. 20005.

Copyright 2005 The Appraisal Foundation.

Appendix 4
Outlines for introductory courses

Appraisal Qualifications Board
Real Property Appraiser Criteria

Core Curriculum

Basic Appraisal Principles (30 HOURS)

A. Residential Property Concepts & Characteristics
    1   Basic Real Property Concepts
    2   Real Property Characteristics
    3   Legal Description (Physical)

B. Legal Consideration
    1   Forms of Ownership
    2   Public and Private Controls
    3   Real Estate Contracts
    4   Leases

C. Influences on Real Estate Values
    1   Governmental
    2   Economic

3   Social

4   Environmental, Geographic and Physical

D.   Types of Value

1   Market Value

2   Other Value Types

E.   Economic Principles

1   Classic Economic Principles

2   Application & Illustration of the Economic Principles

F.   Overview of Real Estate Markets and Analysis

1   Market Fundamentals, Characteristics, and Definitions

2   Supply Analysis

3   Demand Analysis

4   Use of Market Analysis

G.   Ethics and How They Apply in Appraisal Theory and Practice

Basic Appraisal Procedures (30 HOURS)

A.   Overview of Approaches to Value

B.   Valuation Procedures

1   Defining the Problem

2   Collecting and Selecting Data

3   Analyzing

4   Reconciling and Final Value Opinion

5   Communicating the Appraisal

C.   Property Description

1   Geographic Characteristics of the Land/Site

2   Geologic Characteristics of the Land/Site

3   Location and Neighborhood Characteristics

4   Land/Site Considerations for Highest and Best Use

5   Improvements - Architectural Styles and Types of
     Construction

D.   Residential Applications

The 15-Hour National USPAP Course
(or its equivalent)   (15 HOURS)

A.   Preamble and Ethics Rule

B.   Standard 1

C.   Standard 2

D.   Standards 3 to 10

E.   Statements and Advisory Opinions

This outline is reproduced with permission of The Appraisal Foundation, 1029 Vermont Avenue, NW, Suite 900, Washington, D.C. 20005.

Appendix 5
Licensing changes coming in 2008

Should you be considering joining the appraisal business, you should be alert to substantial changes in the federal requirements developed by The Appraisal Foundation for all new appraisers seeking to be licensed beginning January 1, 2008. Check with your state appraisal department to learn about their specific requirements.

In addition to more hours of study, the biggest part of the change is that to become a certified residential appraiser you will need an associate's degree (or the equivalent), and to become a certified general appraiser you will need a bachelor's degree (or the equivalent).

The new requirements follow.

Trainee
Seventy-five hours of appraisal education including:

Basic appraisal principles	30 hours
Basic appraisal procedures	30 hours
15-hour USPAP* course or equivalent	15 hours

*Uniform Standards of Professional Appraisal Practice.

149

Licensed Appraiser (appraisals of one- to four-unit noncomplex residential units having a transaction value of less than $1 million and complex one- to four-unit residential units having a transaction value of less than $250,000)—2,000 hours of experience accumulated over at least a 12-month period.

One hundred and fifty hours of appraisal education that includes:

Basic appraisal principles	30 hours
Basic appraisal procedures	30 hours
15-hour USPAP course (or equivalent)	15 hours
Residential market analysis and highest and best use	15 hours
Residential appraiser site valuation and cost approach	15 hours
Residential sales comparison and income approaches	30 hours
Residential report writing and case studies	15 hours

Certified Residential Appraiser (appraisals of all one- to four-unit residential units regardless of value)–2,500 hours of experience accumulated over at least a 30-month period.

Applicant must hold an associate's degree or higher from an accredited college or shall have completed the following collegiate subjects at an accredited college or university totaling at least 21 semester credit hours:

English composition

Principles of economics (micro or macro)

Finance

Algebra, geometry, or higher mathematics

Statistics

Introduction to computers–word processing/spreadsheets

Business or real estate law

And 200 hours of appraisal education that includes:

Basic appraisal principles	30 hours
Basic appraisal procedures	30 hours

15-hour USPAP course or equivalent	15 hours
Residential market analysis and highest and best use	15 hours
Residential appraiser site valuation and cost approach	15 hours
Residential sales comparison and income approaches	30 hours
Residential report writing and case studies	15 hours
Statistics, modeling, and finance	15 hours
Advanced residential applications and case studies	15 hours
Appraisal subject matter electives	20 hours

Certified General Appraiser (appraisals of all types of real property; it is required that these appraisers comply with the Competency Rule of USPAP)—3,000 hours of experience accumulated over at least a 30-month period.

Applicant must hold a bachelor's degree or higher from an accredited college or shall have completed the following collegiate subjects at an accredited college or university totaling at least 30 semester credit hours:

English composition

Microeconomics

Macroeconomics

Finance

Algebra, geometry, or higher mathematics

Statistics

Introduction to computers–word processing/spreadsheets

Business or real estate law

Two full-credit courses in any two of the following:

Geography

Ageconomics

Accounting

Business management

Real estate

And 300 hours of appraisal education that includes:

Basic appraisal principles	30 hours
Basic appraisal procedures	30 hours
15-hour USPAP course (or its equivalent)	15 hours
General appraiser market analysis and highest and best use	30 hours
Statistics, modeling, and finance	15 hours
General appraiser sales comparison and income approaches	30 hours
General appraiser site valuation and cost approach	30 hours
General appraiser income approach	60 hours
General appraiser report writing and case studies	30 hours
Other appraisal subject matter primary courses	30 hours

These are major changes designed to increase the professionalism of the industry and to ensure that new appraisers have the background they need to do the job.

To find out where tests in your region are held, and who is qualified to teach them, visit your state appraiser Web site. A list of state sites and phone numbers are available in Appendix 8.

Appendix 6
Residential
appraisal forms

The following residential appraisal forms are among the most widely used in the industry.

The copyrighted forms are reproduced with permission of Fannie Mae.

Uniform Residential Appraisal Report   File

The purpose of this summary appraisal report is to provide the lender/client with an accurate, and adequately supported, opinion of the market value of the subject property.

SUBJECT

Property Address		City		State	Zip Code
Borrower		Owner of Public Record		County	
Legal Description					

Assessor's Parcel #		Tax Year	R.E. Taxes $
Neighborhood Name		Map Reference	Census Tract

Occupant ☐ Owner ☐ Tenant ☐ Vacant   Special Assessments $ ☐ PUD HOA $ ☐ per year ☐ per month

Property Rights Appraised ☐ Fee Simple ☐ Leasehold ☐ Other (describe)

Assignment Type ☐ Purchase Transaction ☐ Refinance Transaction ☐ Other (describe)

Lender/Client	Address

Is the subject property currently offered for sale or has it been offered for sale in the twelve months prior to the effective date of this appraisal? ☐ Yes ☐ No

Report data source(s) used, offering price(s), and date(s).

CONTRACT

I ☐ did ☐ did not analyze the contract for sale for the subject purchase transaction. Explain the results of the analysis of the contract for sale or why the analysis was not performed.

Contract Price $ Date of Contract   Is the property seller the owner of public record? ☐ Yes ☐ No Data Source(s)

Is there any financial assistance (loan charges, sale concessions, gift or downpayment assistance, etc.) to be paid by any party on behalf of the borrower? ☐ Yes ☐ No
If Yes, report the total dollar amount and describe the items to be paid.

NEIGHBORHOOD

Note: Race and the racial composition of the neighborhood are not appraisal factors.

Neighborhood Characteristics			One-Unit Housing Trends			One-Unit Housing		Present Land Use %	
Location ☐ Urban ☐ Suburban ☐ Rural			Property Values ☐ Increasing ☐ Stable ☐ Declining			PRICE	AGE	One-Unit	%
Built-Up ☐ Over 75% ☐ 25–75% ☐ Under 25%			Demand/Supply ☐ Shortage ☐ In Balance ☐ Over Supply			$ (000)	(yrs)	2-4 Unit	%
Growth ☐ Rapid ☐ Stable ☐ Slow			Marketing Time ☐ Under 3 mths ☐ 3–6 mths ☐ Over 6 mths			Low		Multi-Family	%
Neighborhood Boundaries						High		Commercial	%
						Pred.		Other	%

Neighborhood Description

Market Conditions (including support for the above conclusions)

SITE

Dimensions		Area	Shape	View
Specific Zoning Classification		Zoning Description		

Zoning Compliance ☐ Legal ☐ Legal Nonconforming (Grandfathered Use) ☐ No Zoning ☐ Illegal (describe)

Is the highest and best use of the subject property as improved (or as proposed per plans and specifications) the present use? ☐ Yes ☐ No If No, describe

Utilities	Public	Other (describe)		Public	Other (describe)	Off-site Improvements—Type	Public	Private
Electricity	☐	☐	Water	☐	☐	Street	☐	☐
Gas	☐	☐	Sanitary Sewer	☐	☐	Alley	☐	☐

FEMA Special Flood Hazard Area ☐ Yes ☐ No FEMA Flood Zone   FEMA Map #   FEMA Map Date

Are the utilities and off-site improvements typical for the market area? ☐ Yes ☐ No If No, describe

Are there any adverse site conditions or external factors (easements, encroachments, environmental conditions, land uses, etc.)? ☐ Yes ☐ No If Yes, describe

IMPROVEMENTS

General Description		Foundation		Exterior Description	materials/condition	Interior	materials/condition
Units ☐ One ☐ One with Accessory Unit		☐ Concrete Slab ☐ Crawl Space		Foundation Walls		Floors	
# of Stories		☐ Full Basement ☐ Partial Basement		Exterior Walls		Walls	
Type ☐ Det. ☐ Att. ☐ S-Det./End Unit		Basement Area sq. ft.		Roof Surface		Trim/Finish	
☐ Existing ☐ Proposed ☐ Under Const.		Basement Finish %		Gutters & Downspouts		Bath Floor	
Design (Style)		☐ Outside Entry/Exit ☐ Sump Pump		Window Type		Bath Wainscot	
Year Built		Evidence of ☐ Infestation		Storm Sash/Insulated		Car Storage ☐ None	
Effective Age (Yrs)		☐ Dampness ☐ Settlement		Screens		Driveway # of Cars	
Attic ☐ None		Heating ☐ FWA ☐ HWBB ☐ Radiant		Amenities ☐ Woodstove(s) #		Driveway Surface	
☐ Drop Stair ☐ Stairs		☐ Other Fuel		☐ Fireplace(s) # ☐ Fence		☐ Garage # of Cars	
☐ Floor ☐ Scuttle		Cooling ☐ Central Air Conditioning		☐ Patio/Deck ☐ Porch		☐ Carport # of Cars	
☐ Finished ☐ Heated		☐ Individual ☐ Other		☐ Pool ☐ Other		☐ Att. ☐ Det. ☐ Built-in	

Appliances ☐ Refrigerator ☐ Range/Oven ☐ Dishwasher ☐ Disposal ☐ Microwave ☐ Washer/Dryer ☐ Other (describe)

Finished area above grade contains: Rooms Bedrooms Bath(s) Square Feet of Gross Living Area Above Grade

Additional features (special energy efficient items, etc.).

Describe the condition of the property (including needed repairs, deterioration, renovations, remodeling, etc.).

Are there any physical deficiencies or adverse conditions that affect the livability, soundness, or structural integrity of the property? ☐ Yes ☐ No If Yes, describe

Does the property generally conform to the neighborhood (functional utility, style, condition, use, construction, etc.)? ☐ Yes ☐ No If No, describe

Residential appraisal forms

Uniform Residential Appraisal Report

File #

There are ___ comparable properties currently offered for sale in the subject neighborhood ranging in price from $ ___ to $ ___						
There are ___ comparable sales in the subject neighborhood within the past twelve months ranging in sale price from $ ___ to $ ___						

FEATURE	SUBJECT	COMPARABLE SALE # 1		COMPARABLE SALE # 2		COMPARABLE SALE # 3	
Address							
Proximity to Subject							
Sale Price	$		$		$		$
Sale Price/Gross Liv. Area	$ ___ sq. ft.	$ ___ sq. ft.		$ ___ sq. ft.		$ ___ sq. ft.	
Data Source(s)							
Verification Source(s)							
VALUE ADJUSTMENTS	DESCRIPTION	DESCRIPTION	+(-) $ Adjustment	DESCRIPTION	+(-) $ Adjustment	DESCRIPTION	+(-) $ Adjustment
Sale or Financing Concessions							
Date of Sale/Time							
Location							
Leasehold/Fee Simple							
Site							
View							
Design (Style)							
Quality of Construction							
Actual Age							
Condition							
Above Grade	Total Bdrms. Baths	Total Bdrms. Baths		Total Bdrms. Baths		Total Bdrms. Baths	
Room Count							
Gross Living Area	sq. ft.	sq. ft.		sq. ft.		sq. ft.	
Basement & Finished Rooms Below Grade							
Functional Utility							
Heating/Cooling							
Energy Efficient Items							
Garage/Carport							
Porch/Patio/Deck							
Net Adjustment (Total)		☐ + ☐ -	$	☐ + ☐ -	$	☐ + ☐ -	$
Adjusted Sale Price of Comparables		Net Adj. ___ % Gross Adj. ___ %	$	Net Adj. ___ % Gross Adj. ___ %	$	Net Adj. ___ % Gross Adj. ___ %	$

(Left margin vertical label: S A L E S   C O M P A R I S O N   A P P R O A C H)

I ☐ did ☐ did not research the sale or transfer history of the subject property and comparable sales. If not, explain

My research ☐ did ☐ did not reveal any prior sales or transfers of the subject property for the three years prior to the effective date of this appraisal.

Data source(s)

My research ☐ did ☐ did not reveal any prior sales or transfers of the comparable sales for the year prior to the date of sale of the comparable sale.

Data source(s)

Report the results of the research and analysis of the prior sale or transfer history of the subject property and comparable sales (report additional prior sales on page 3).

ITEM	SUBJECT	COMPARABLE SALE # 1	COMPARABLE SALE # 2	COMPARABLE SALE # 3
Date of Prior Sale/Transfer				
Price of Prior Sale/Transfer				
Data Source(s)				
Effective Date of Data Source(s)				

Analysis of prior sale or transfer history of the subject property and comparable sales

Summary of Sales Comparison Approach

Indicated Value by Sales Comparison Approach $

Indicated Value by: Sales Comparison Approach $ ___   Cost Approach (if developed) $ ___   Income Approach (if developed) $ ___

(Left margin vertical label: R E C O N C I L I A T I O N)

This appraisal is made ☐ "as is", ☐ subject to completion per plans and specifications on the basis of a hypothetical condition that the improvements have been completed, ☐ subject to the following repairs or alterations on the basis of a hypothetical condition that the repairs or alterations have been completed, or ☐ subject to the following required inspection based on the extraordinary assumption that the condition or deficiency does not require alteration or repair:

Based on a complete visual inspection of the interior and exterior areas of the subject property, defined scope of work, statement of assumptions and limiting conditions, and appraiser's certification, my (our) opinion of the market value, as defined, of the real property that is the subject of this report is $ ___ , as of ___ , which is the date of inspection and the effective date of this appraisal.

Uniform Residential Appraisal Report

File #

ADDITIONAL COMMENTS

COST APPROACH

COST APPROACH TO VALUE (not required by Fannie Mae)

Provide adequate information for the lender/client to replicate the below cost figures and calculations.

Support for the opinion of site value (summary of comparable land sales or other methods for estimating site value)

ESTIMATED ☐ REPRODUCTION OR ☐ REPLACEMENT COST NEW	OPINION OF SITE VALUE = $
Source of cost data	Dwelling Sq. Ft. @ $ =$
Quality rating from cost service Effective date of cost data	Sq. Ft. @ $ =$
Comments on Cost Approach (gross living area calculations, depreciation, etc.)	
	Garage/Carport Sq. Ft. @ $ =$
	Total Estimate of Cost-New = $
	Less Physical / Functional / External
	Depreciation =$( )
	Depreciated Cost of Improvements =$
	"As-is" Value of Site Improvements =$
Estimated Remaining Economic Life (HUD and VA only) Years	Indicated Value By Cost Approach =$

INCOME

INCOME APPROACH TO VALUE (not required by Fannie Mae)

Estimated Monthly Market Rent $ X Gross Rent Multiplier = $ Indicated Value by Income Approach

Summary of Income Approach (including support for market rent and GRM)

PUD INFORMATION

PROJECT INFORMATION FOR PUDs (if applicable)

Is the developer/builder in control of the Homeowners' Association (HOA)? ☐ Yes ☐ No Unit type(s) ☐ Detached ☐ Attached

Provide the following information for PUDs ONLY if the developer/builder is in control of the HOA and the subject property is an attached dwelling unit.

Legal name of project

Total number of phases Total number of units Total number of units sold

Total number of units rented Total number of units for sale Data source(s)

Was the project created by the conversion of an existing building(s) into a PUD? ☐ Yes ☐ No If Yes, date of conversion

Does the project contain any multi-dwelling units? ☐ Yes ☐ No Data source(s)

Are the units, common elements, and recreation facilities complete? ☐ Yes ☐ No If No, describe the status of completion.

Are the common elements leased to or by the Homeowners' Association? ☐ Yes ☐ No If Yes, describe the rental terms and options.

Describe common elements and recreational facilities

Freddie Mac Form 70 March 2005 Page 3 of 6 Fannie Mae Form 1004 March 2005

Residential appraisal forms

Uniform Residential Appraisal Report

File #

This report form is designed to report an appraisal of a one-unit property or a one-unit property with an accessory unit; including a unit in a planned unit development (PUD). This report form is not designed to report an appraisal of a manufactured home or a unit in a condominium or cooperative project.

This appraisal report is subject to the following scope of work, intended use, intended user, definition of market value, statement of assumptions and limiting conditions, and certifications. Modifications, additions, or deletions to the intended use, intended user, definition of market value, or assumptions and limiting conditions are not permitted. The appraiser may expand the scope of work to include any additional research or analysis necessary based on the complexity of this appraisal assignment. Modifications or deletions to the certifications are also not permitted. However, additional certifications that do not constitute material alterations to this appraisal report, such as those required by law or those related to the appraiser's continuing education or membership in an appraisal organization, are permitted.

SCOPE OF WORK: The scope of work for this appraisal is defined by the complexity of this appraisal assignment and the reporting requirements of this appraisal report form, including the following definition of market value, statement of assumptions and limiting conditions, and certifications. The appraiser must, at a minimum: (1) perform a complete visual inspection of the interior and exterior areas of the subject property, (2) inspect the neighborhood, (3) inspect each of the comparable sales from at least the street, (4) research, verify, and analyze data from reliable public and/or private sources, and (5) report his or her analysis, opinions, and conclusions in this appraisal report.

INTENDED USE: The intended use of this appraisal report is for the lender/client to evaluate the property that is the subject of this appraisal for a mortgage finance transaction.

INTENDED USER: The intended user of this appraisal report is the lender/client.

DEFINITION OF MARKET VALUE: The most probable price which a property should bring in a competitive and open market under all conditions requisite to a fair sale, the buyer and seller, each acting prudently, knowledgeably and assuming the price is not affected by undue stimulus. Implicit in this definition is the consummation of a sale as of a specified date and the passing of title from seller to buyer under conditions whereby: (1) buyer and seller are typically motivated; (2) both parties are well informed or well advised, and each acting in what he or she considers his or her own best interest; (3) a reasonable time is allowed for exposure in the open market; (4) payment is made in terms of cash in U. S. dollars or in terms of financial arrangements comparable thereto; and (5) the price represents the normal consideration for the property sold unaffected by special or creative financing or sales concessions* granted by anyone associated with the sale.

*Adjustments to the comparables must be made for special or creative financing or sales concessions. No adjustments are necessary for those costs which are normally paid by sellers as a result of tradition or law in a market area; these costs are readily identifiable since the seller pays these costs in virtually all sales transactions. Special or creative financing adjustments can be made to the comparable property by comparisons to financing terms offered by a third party institutional lender that is not already involved in the property or transaction. Any adjustment should not be calculated on a mechanical dollar for dollar cost of the financing or concession but the dollar amount of any adjustment should approximate the market's reaction to the financing or concessions based on the appraiser's judgment.

STATEMENT OF ASSUMPTIONS AND LIMITING CONDITIONS: The appraiser's certification in this report is subject to the following assumptions and limiting conditions:

1. The appraiser will not be responsible for matters of a legal nature that affect either the property being appraised or the title to it, except for information that he or she became aware of during the research involved in performing this appraisal. The appraiser assumes that the title is good and marketable and will not render any opinions about the title.

2. The appraiser has provided a sketch in this appraisal report to show the approximate dimensions of the improvements. The sketch is included only to assist the reader in visualizing the property and understanding the appraiser's determination of its size.

3. The appraiser has examined the available flood maps that are provided by the Federal Emergency Management Agency (or other data sources) and has noted in this appraisal report whether any portion of the subject site is located in an identified Special Flood Hazard Area. Because the appraiser is not a surveyor, he or she makes no guarantees, express or implied, regarding this determination.

4. The appraiser will not give testimony or appear in court because he or she made an appraisal of the property in question, unless specific arrangements to do so have been made beforehand, or as otherwise required by law.

5. The appraiser has noted in this appraisal report any adverse conditions (such as needed repairs, deterioration, the presence of hazardous wastes, toxic substances, etc.) observed during the inspection of the subject property or that he or she became aware of during the research involved in performing this appraisal. Unless otherwise stated in this appraisal report, the appraiser has no knowledge of any hidden or unapparent physical deficiencies or adverse conditions of the property (such as, but not limited to, needed repairs, deterioration, the presence of hazardous wastes, toxic substances, adverse environmental conditions, etc.) that would make the property less valuable, and has assumed that there are no such conditions and makes no guarantees or warranties, express or implied. The appraiser will not be responsible for any such conditions that do exist or for any engineering or testing that might be required to discover whether such conditions exist. Because the appraiser is not an expert in the field of environmental hazards, this appraisal report must not be considered as an environmental assessment of the property.

6. The appraiser has based his or her appraisal report and valuation conclusion for an appraisal that is subject to satisfactory completion, repairs, or alterations on the assumption that the completion, repairs, or alterations of the subject property will be performed in a professional manner.

Appendixes

Uniform Residential Appraisal Report File

APPRAISER'S CERTIFICATION: The Appraiser certifies and agrees that:

1. I have, at a minimum, developed and reported this appraisal in accordance with the scope of work requirements stated in this appraisal report.

2. I performed a complete visual inspection of the interior and exterior areas of the subject property. I reported the condition of the improvements in factual, specific terms. I identified and reported the physical deficiencies that could affect the livability, soundness, or structural integrity of the property.

3. I performed this appraisal in accordance with the requirements of the Uniform Standards of Professional Appraisal Practice that were adopted and promulgated by the Appraisal Standards Board of The Appraisal Foundation and that were in place at the time this appraisal report was prepared.

4. I developed my opinion of the market value of the real property that is the subject of this report based on the sales comparison approach to value. I have adequate comparable market data to develop a reliable sales comparison approach for this appraisal assignment. I further certify that I considered the cost and income approaches to value but did not develop them, unless otherwise indicated in this report.

5. I researched, verified, analyzed, and reported on any current agreement for sale for the subject property, any offering for sale of the subject property in the twelve months prior to the effective date of this appraisal, and the prior sales of the subject property for a minimum of three years prior to the effective date of this appraisal, unless otherwise indicated in this report.

6. I researched, verified, analyzed, and reported on the prior sales of the comparable sales for a minimum of one year prior to the date of sale of the comparable sale, unless otherwise indicated in this report.

7. I selected and used comparable sales that are locationally, physically, and functionally the most similar to the subject property.

8. I have not used comparable sales that were the result of combining a land sale with the contract purchase price of a home that has been built or will be built on the land.

9. I have reported adjustments to the comparable sales that reflect the market's reaction to the differences between the subject property and the comparable sales.

10. I verified, from a disinterested source, all information in this report that was provided by parties who have a financial interest in the sale or financing of the subject property.

11. I have knowledge and experience in appraising this type of property in this market area.

12. I am aware of, and have access to, the necessary and appropriate public and private data sources, such as multiple listing services, tax assessment records, public land records and other such data sources for the area in which the property is located.

13. I obtained the information, estimates, and opinions furnished by other parties and expressed in this appraisal report from reliable sources that I believe to be true and correct.

14. I have taken into consideration the factors that have an impact on value with respect to the subject neighborhood, subject property, and the proximity of the subject property to adverse influences in the development of my opinion of market value. I have noted in this appraisal report any adverse conditions (such as, but not limited to, needed repairs, deterioration, the presence of hazardous wastes, toxic substances, adverse environmental conditions, etc.) observed during the inspection of the subject property or that I became aware of during the research involved in performing this appraisal. I have considered these adverse conditions in my analysis of the property value, and have reported on the effect of the conditions on the value and marketability of the subject property.

15. I have not knowingly withheld any significant information from this appraisal report and, to the best of my knowledge, all statements and information in this appraisal report are true and correct.

16. I stated in this appraisal report my own personal, unbiased, and professional analysis, opinions, and conclusions, which are subject only to the assumptions and limiting conditions in this appraisal report.

17. I have no present or prospective interest in the property that is the subject of this report, and I have no present or prospective personal interest or bias with respect to the participants in the transaction. I did not base, either partially or completely, my analysis and/or opinion of market value in this appraisal report on the race, color, religion, sex, age, marital status, handicap, familial status, or national origin of either the prospective owners or occupants of the subject property or of the present owners or occupants of the properties in the vicinity of the subject property or on any other basis prohibited by law.

18. My employment and/or compensation for performing this appraisal or any future or anticipated appraisals was not conditioned on any agreement or understanding, written or otherwise, that I would report (or present analysis supporting) a predetermined specific value, a predetermined minimum value, a range or direction in value, a value that favors the cause of any party, or the attainment of a specific result or occurrence of a specific subsequent event (such as approval of a pending mortgage loan application).

19. I personally prepared all conclusions and opinions about the real estate that were set forth in this appraisal report. If I relied on significant real property appraisal assistance from any individual or individuals in the performance of this appraisal or the preparation of this appraisal report, I have named such individual(s) and disclosed the specific tasks performed in this appraisal report. I certify that any individual so named is qualified to perform the tasks. I have not authorized anyone to make a change to any item in this appraisal report; therefore, any change made to this appraisal is unauthorized and I will take no responsibility for it.

20. I identified the lender/client in this appraisal report who is the individual, organization, or agent for the organization that ordered and will receive this appraisal report.

Residential appraisal forms

Uniform Residential Appraisal Report   File

21. The lender/client may disclose or distribute this appraisal report to: the borrower; another lender at the request of the borrower; the mortgagee or its successors and assigns; mortgage insurers; government sponsored enterprises; other secondary market participants; data collection or reporting services; professional appraisal organizations; any department, agency, or instrumentality of the United States; and any state, the District of Columbia, or other jurisdictions; without having to obtain the appraiser's or supervisory appraiser's (if applicable) consent. Such consent must be obtained before this appraisal report may be disclosed or distributed to any other party (including, but not limited to, the public through advertising, public relations, news, sales, or other media).

22. I am aware that any disclosure or distribution of this appraisal report by me or the lender/client may be subject to certain laws and regulations. Further, I am also subject to the provisions of the Uniform Standards of Professional Appraisal Practice that pertain to disclosure or distribution by me.

23. The borrower, another lender at the request of the borrower, the mortgagee or its successors and assigns, mortgage insurers, government sponsored enterprises, and other secondary market participants may rely on this appraisal report as part of any mortgage finance transaction that involves any one or more of these parties.

24. If this appraisal report was transmitted as an "electronic record" containing my "electronic signature," as those terms are defined in applicable federal and/or state laws (excluding audio and video recordings), or a facsimile transmission of this appraisal report containing a copy or representation of my signature, the appraisal report shall be as effective, enforceable and valid as if a paper version of this appraisal report were delivered containing my original hand written signature.

25. Any intentional or negligent misrepresentation(s) contained in this appraisal report may result in civil liability and/or criminal penalties including, but not limited to, fine or imprisonment or both under the provisions of Title 18, United States Code, Section 1001, et seq., or similar state laws.

SUPERVISORY APPRAISER'S CERTIFICATION: The Supervisory Appraiser certifies and agrees that:

1. I directly supervised the appraiser for this appraisal assignment, have read the appraisal report, and agree with the appraiser's analysis, opinions, statements, conclusions, and the appraiser's certification.

2. I accept full responsibility for the contents of this appraisal report including, but not limited to, the appraiser's analysis, opinions, statements, conclusions, and the appraiser's certification.

3. The appraiser identified in this appraisal report is either a sub-contractor or an employee of the supervisory appraiser (or the appraisal firm), is qualified to perform this appraisal, and is acceptable to perform this appraisal under the applicable state law.

4. This appraisal report complies with the Uniform Standards of Professional Appraisal Practice that were adopted and promulgated by the Appraisal Standards Board of The Appraisal Foundation and that were in place at the time this appraisal report was prepared.

5. If this appraisal report was transmitted as an "electronic record" containing my "electronic signature," as those terms are defined in applicable federal and/or state laws (excluding audio and video recordings), or a facsimile transmission of this appraisal report containing a copy or representation of my signature, the appraisal report shall be as effective, enforceable and valid as if a paper version of this appraisal report were delivered containing my original hand written signature.

APPRAISER	SUPERVISORY APPRAISER (ONLY IF REQUIRED)
Signature_____	Signature_____
Name _____	Name_____
Company Name _____	Company Name _____
Company Address_____	Company Address_____
Telephone Number _____	Telephone Number _____
Email Address _____	Email Address _____
Date of Signature and Report_____	Date of Signature _____
Effective Date of Appraisal _____	State Certification # _____
State Certification #_____	or State License # _____
or State License # _____	State _____
or Other (describe) _____ State # _____	Expiration Date of Certification or License _____
State _____	
Expiration Date of Certification or License _____	**SUBJECT PROPERTY**
	☐ Did not inspect subject property
ADDRESS OF PROPERTY APPRAISED	☐ Did inspect exterior of subject property from street
_____	Date of Inspection _____
_____	☐ Did inspect interior and exterior of subject property
APPRAISED VALUE OF SUBJECT PROPERTY $ _____	Date of Inspection _____
LENDER/CLIENT	
Name _____	**COMPARABLE SALES**
Company Name _____	
Company Address_____	☐ Did not inspect exterior of comparable sales from street
_____	☐ Did inspect exterior of comparable sales from street
Email Address _____	Date of Inspection _____

Appendixes

Exterior-Only Inspection Residential Appraisal Report

File #

The purpose of this summary appraisal report is to provide the lender/client with an accurate, and adequately supported, opinion of the market value of the subject property.

Property Address		City		State	Zip Code
Borrower		Owner of Public Record		County	

Legal Description

Assessor's Parcel #		Tax Year	R.E. Taxes $
Neighborhood Name		Map Reference	Census Tract

Occupant ☐ Owner ☐ Tenant ☐ Vacant   Special Assessments $ ☐ PUD   HOA $ ☐ per year ☐ per month

Property Rights Appraised ☐ Fee Simple ☐ Leasehold ☐ Other (describe)

Assignment Type ☐ Purchase Transaction ☐ Refinance Transaction ☐ Other (describe)

Lender/Client		Address	

Is the subject property currently offered for sale or has it been offered for sale in the twelve months prior to the effective date of this appraisal? ☐ Yes ☐ No

Report data source(s) used, offering price(s), and date(s).

I ☐ did ☐ did not analyze the contract for sale for the subject purchase transaction. Explain the results of the analysis of the contract for sale or why the analysis was not performed.

Contract Price $ Date of Contract   Is the property seller the owner of public record? ☐ Yes ☐ No Data Source(s)

Is there any financial assistance (loan charges, sale concessions, gift or downpayment assistance, etc.) to be paid by any party on behalf of the borrower? ☐ Yes ☐ No
If Yes, report the total dollar amount and describe the items to be paid.

Note: Race and the racial composition of the neighborhood are not appraisal factors.

Neighborhood Characteristics			One-Unit Housing Trends			One-Unit Housing		Present Land Use %	
Location ☐ Urban ☐ Suburban ☐ Rural			Property Values ☐ Increasing ☐ Stable ☐ Declining			PRICE	AGE	One-Unit	%
Built-Up ☐ Over 75% ☐ 25–75% ☐ Under 25%			Demand/Supply ☐ Shortage ☐ In Balance ☐ Over Supply			$ (000)	(yrs)	2-4 Unit	%
Growth ☐ Rapid ☐ Stable ☐ Slow			Marketing Time ☐ Under 3 mths ☐ 3–6 mths ☐ Over 6 mths			Low		Multi-Family	%
Neighborhood Boundaries						High		Commercial	%
						Pred.		Other	%

Neighborhood Description

Market Conditions (including support for the above conclusions)

Dimensions		Area		Shape		View	
Specific Zoning Classification		Zoning Description					

Zoning Compliance ☐ Legal ☐ Legal Nonconforming (Grandfathered Use) ☐ No Zoning ☐ Illegal (describe)

Is the highest and best use of the subject property as improved (or as proposed per plans and specifications) the present use? ☐ Yes ☐ No If No, describe

Utilities	Public	Other (describe)		Public	Other (describe)		Off-site Improvements—Type	Public	Private
Electricity	☐	☐	Water	☐	☐		Street	☐	☐
Gas	☐	☐	Sanitary Sewer	☐	☐		Alley	☐	☐

FEMA Special Flood Hazard Area ☐ Yes ☐ No FEMA Flood Zone   FEMA Map #   FEMA Map Date

Are the utilities and off-site improvements typical for the market area? ☐ Yes ☐ No If No, describe

Are there any adverse site conditions or external factors (easements, encroachments, environmental conditions, land uses, etc.)? ☐ Yes ☐ No If Yes, describe

Source(s) Used for Physical Characteristics of Property ☐ Appraisal Files ☐ MLS ☐ Assessment and Tax Records ☐ Prior Inspection ☐ Property Owner
☐ Other (describe)   Data Source(s) for Gross Living Area

General Description		General Description		Heating / Cooling	Amenities		Car Storage	
Units ☐ One ☐ One with Accessory Unit		☐ Concrete Slab ☐ Crawl Space		☐ FWA ☐ HWBB	☐ Fireplace(s) #		☐ None	
# of Stories		☐ Full Basement ☐ Finished		☐ Radiant	☐ Woodstove(s) #		☐ Driveway	# of Cars
Type ☐ Det. ☐ Att. ☐ S-Det./End Unit		☐ Partial Basement ☐ Finished		☐ Other	☐ Patio/Deck		Driveway Surface	
☐ Existing ☐ Proposed ☐ Under Const.	Exterior Walls			Fuel	☐ Porch		☐ Garage	# of Cars
Design (Style)	Roof Surface			☐ Central Air Conditioning	☐ Pool		☐ Carport	# of Cars
Year Built	Gutters & Downspouts			☐ Individual	☐ Fence		☐ Attached ☐ Detached	
Effective Age (Yrs)	Window Type			☐ Other	☐ Other		☐ Built-in	

Appliances ☐ Refrigerator ☐ Range/Oven ☐ Dishwasher ☐ Disposal ☐ Microwave ☐ Washer/Dryer ☐ Other (describe)

Finished area **above** grade contains:	Rooms	Bedrooms	Bath(s)	Square Feet of Gross Living Area Above Grade

Additional features (special energy efficient items, etc.)

Describe the condition of the property and data source(s) (including apparent needed repairs, deterioration, renovations, remodeling, etc.).

Are there any apparent physical deficiencies or adverse conditions that affect the livability, soundness, or structural integrity of the property? ☐ Yes ☐ No
If Yes, describe

Does the property generally conform to the neighborhood (functional utility, style, condition, use, construction, etc.)? ☐ Yes ☐ No If No, describe

Freddie Mac Form 2055 March 2005   Page 1 of 6   Fannie Mae Form 2055 March 2005

160

Residential appraisal forms

Exterior-Only Inspection Residential Appraisal Report   File

| There are | comparable properties currently offered for sale in the subject neighborhood ranging in price from $ | | to $ | |
| There are | comparable sales in the subject neighborhood within the past twelve months ranging in sale price from $ | | to $ | |

FEATURE	SUBJECT	COMPARABLE SALE # 1		COMPARABLE SALE # 2		COMPARABLE SALE # 3	
Address							
Proximity to Subject							
Sale Price	$		$		$		$
Sale Price/Gross Liv. Area	$ sq. ft.	$ sq. ft.		$ sq. ft.		$ sq. ft.	
Data Source(s)							
Verification Source(s)							
VALUE ADJUSTMENTS	DESCRIPTION	DESCRIPTION	+(-) $ Adjustment	DESCRIPTION	+(-) $ Adjustment	DESCRIPTION	+(-) $ Adjustment
Sale or Financing Concessions							
Date of Sale/Time							
Location							
Leasehold/Fee Simple							
Site							
View							
Design (Style)							
Quality of Construction							
Actual Age							
Condition							
Above Grade	Total Bdrms. Baths	Total Bdrms. Baths		Total Bdrms. Baths		Total Bdrms. Baths	
Room Count							
Gross Living Area	sq. ft.	sq. ft.		sq. ft.		sq. ft.	
Basement & Finished Rooms Below Grade							
Functional Utility							
Heating/Cooling							
Energy Efficient Items							
Garage/Carport							
Porch/Patio/Deck							
Net Adjustment (Total)		☐ + ☐ -	$	☐ + ☐ -	$	☐ + ☐ -	$
Adjusted Sale Price of Comparables		Net Adj. % Gross Adj. %	$	Net Adj. % Gross Adj. %	$	Net Adj. % Gross Adj. %	$

I ☐ did ☐ did not research the sale or transfer history of the subject property and comparable sales. If not, explain

My research ☐ did ☐ did not reveal any prior sales or transfers of the subject property for the three years prior to the effective date of this appraisal.
Data source(s)
My research ☐ did ☐ did not reveal any prior sales or transfers of the comparable sales for the year prior to the date of sale of the comparable sale.
Data source(s)
Report the results of the research and analysis of the prior sale or transfer history of the subject property and comparable sales (report additional prior sales on page 3).

ITEM	SUBJECT	COMPARABLE SALE # 1	COMPARABLE SALE # 2	COMPARABLE SALE # 3
Date of Prior Sale/Transfer				
Price of Prior Sale/Transfer				
Data Source(s)				
Effective Date of Data Source(s)				

Analysis of prior sale or transfer history of the subject property and comparable sales

Summary of Sales Comparison Approach

Indicated Value by Sales Comparison Approach $

Indicated Value by: Sales Comparison Approach $ Cost Approach (if developed) $ Income Approach (if developed) $

This appraisal is made ☐ "as is", ☐ subject to completion per plans and specifications on the basis of a hypothetical condition that the improvements have been completed, ☐ subject to the following repairs or alterations on the basis of a hypothetical condition that the repairs or alterations have been completed, or ☐ subject to the following required inspection based on the extraordinary assumption that the condition or deficiency does not require alteration or repair:

Based on a visual inspection of the exterior areas of the subject property from at least the street, defined scope of work, statement of assumptions and limiting conditions, and appraiser's certification, my (our) opinion of the market value, as defined, of the real property that is the subject of this report is
$, as of   , which is the date of the inspection and the effective date of this appraisal.

Appendixes

Exterior-Only Inspection Residential Appraisal Report

File #

ADDITIONAL COMMENTS

COST APPROACH TO VALUE (not required by Fannie Mae)

Provide adequate information for the lender/client to replicate the below cost figures and calculations.

Support for the opinion of site value (summary of comparable land sales or other methods for estimating site value)

ESTIMATED ☐ REPRODUCTION OR ☐ REPLACEMENT COST NEW	OPINION OF SITE VALUE..= $
Source of cost data	Dwelling Sq. Ft. @ $ =$
Quality rating from cost service Effective date of cost data	Sq. Ft. @ $ =$
Comments on Cost Approach (gross living area calculations, depreciation, etc.)	Garage/Carport Sq. Ft. @ $ =$
	Total Estimate of Cost-New = $
	Less Physical Functional External
	Depreciation =$( )
	Depreciated Cost of Improvements............................=$
	"As-is" Value of Site Improvements.............................=$
Estimated Remaining Economic Life (HUD and VA only) Years	Indicated Value By Cost Approach...=$

COST APPROACH

INCOME APPROACH TO VALUE (not required by Fannie Mae)

Estimated Monthly Market Rent $ X Gross Rent Multiplier   = $ Indicated Value by Income Approach

Summary of Income Approach (including support for market rent and GRM)

INCOME

PROJECT INFORMATION FOR PUDs (if applicable)

Is the developer/builder in control of the Homeowners' Association (HOA)? ☐ Yes ☐ No   Unit type(s) ☐ Detached ☐ Attached

Provide the following information for PUDs ONLY if the developer/builder is in control of the HOA and the subject property is an attached dwelling unit.

Legal name of project

Total number of phases	Total number of units	Total number of units sold
Total number of units rented	Total number of units for sale	Data source(s)

Was the project created by the conversion of an existing building(s) into a PUD? ☐ Yes ☐ No If Yes, date of conversion

Does the project contain any multi-dwelling units? ☐ Yes ☐ No Data source(s)

Are the units, common elements, and recreation facilities complete? ☐ Yes ☐ No If No, describe the status of completion.

Are the common elements leased to or by the Homeowners' Association? ☐ Yes ☐ No If Yes, describe the rental terms and options.

Describe common elements and recreational facilities

PUD INFORMATION

Residential appraisal forms

Exterior-Only Inspection Residential Appraisal Report File

This report form is designed to report an appraisal of a one-unit property or a one-unit property with an accessory unit; including a unit in a planned unit development (PUD). This report form is not designed to report an appraisal of a manufactured home or a unit in a condominium or cooperative project.

This appraisal report is subject to the following scope of work, intended use, intended user, definition of market value, statement of assumptions and limiting conditions, and certifications. Modifications, additions, or deletions to the intended use, intended user, definition of market value, or assumptions and limiting conditions are not permitted. The appraiser may expand the scope of work to include any additional research or analysis necessary based on the complexity of this appraisal assignment. Modifications or deletions to the certifications are also not permitted. However, additional certifications that do not constitute material alterations to this appraisal report, such as those required by law or those related to the appraiser's continuing education or membership in an appraisal organization, are permitted.

SCOPE OF WORK: The scope of work for this appraisal is defined by the complexity of this appraisal assignment and the reporting requirements of this appraisal report form, including the following definition of market value, statement of assumptions and limiting conditions, and certifications. The appraiser must, at a minimum: (1) perform a visual inspection of the exterior areas of the subject property from at least the street, (2) inspect the neighborhood, (3) inspect each of the comparable sales from at least the street, (4) research, verify, and analyze data from reliable public and/or private sources, and (5) report his or her analysis, opinions, and conclusions in this appraisal report.

The appraiser must be able to obtain adequate information about the physical characteristics (including, but not limited to, condition, room count, gross living area, etc.) of the subject property from the exterior-only inspection and reliable public and/or private sources to perform this appraisal. The appraiser should use the same type of data sources that he or she uses for comparable sales such as, but not limited to, multiple listing services, tax and assessment records, prior inspections, appraisal files, information provided by the property owner, etc.

INTENDED USE: The intended use of this appraisal report is for the lender/client to evaluate the property that is the subject of this appraisal for a mortgage finance transaction.

INTENDED USER: The intended user of this appraisal report is the lender/client.

DEFINITION MARKET VALUE: The most probable price which a property should bring in a competitive and open market under all conditions requisite to a fair sale, the buyer and seller, each acting prudently, knowledgeably and assuming the price is not affected by undue stimulus. Implicit in this definition is the consummation of a sale as of a specified date and the passing of title from seller to buyer under conditions whereby: (1) buyer and seller are typically motivated; (2) both parties are well informed or well advised, and each acting in what he or she considers his or her own best interest; (3) a reasonable time is allowed for exposure in the open market; (4) payment is made in terms of cash in U. S. dollars or in terms of financial arrangements comparable thereto; and (5) the price represents the normal consideration for the property sold unaffected by special or creative financing or sales concessions* granted by anyone associated with the sale.

*Adjustments to the comparables must be made for special or creative financing or sales concessions. No adjustments are necessary for those costs which are normally paid by sellers as a result of tradition or law in a market area; these costs are readily identifiable since the seller pays these costs in virtually all sales transactions. Special or creative financing adjustments can be made to the comparable property by comparisons to financing terms offered by a third party institutional lender that is not already involved in the property or transaction. Any adjustment should not be calculated on a mechanical dollar for dollar cost of the financing or concession but the dollar amount of any adjustment should approximate the market's reaction to the financing or concessions based on the appraiser's judgment.

STATEMENT OF ASSUMPTIONS AND LIMITING CONDITIONS: The appraiser's certification in this report is subject to the following assumptions and limiting conditions:

1. The appraiser will not be responsible for matters of a legal nature that affect either the property being appraised or the title to it, except for information that he or she became aware of during the research involved in performing this appraisal. The appraiser assumes that the title is good and marketable and will not render any opinions about the title.

2. The appraiser has examined the available flood maps that are provided by the Federal Emergency Management Agency (or other data sources) and has noted in this appraisal report whether any portion of the subject site is located in an identified Special Flood Hazard Area. Because the appraiser is not a surveyor, he or she makes no guarantees, express or implied, regarding this determination.

3. The appraiser will not give testimony or appear in court because he or she made an appraisal of the property in question, unless specific arrangements to do so have been made beforehand, or as otherwise required by law.

4. The appraiser has noted in this appraisal report any adverse conditions (such as needed repairs, deterioration, the presence of hazardous wastes, toxic substances, etc.) observed during the inspection of the subject property or that he or she became aware of during the research involved in performing this appraisal. Unless otherwise stated in this appraisal report, the appraiser has no knowledge of any hidden or unapparent physical deficiencies or adverse conditions of the property (such as, but not limited to, needed repairs, deterioration, the presence of hazardous wastes, toxic substances, adverse environmental conditions, etc.) that would make the property less valuable, and has assumed that there are no such conditions and makes no guarantees or warranties, express or implied. The appraiser will not be responsible for any such conditions that do exist or for any engineering or testing that might be required to discover whether such conditions exist. Because the appraiser is not an expert in the field of environmental hazards, this appraisal report must not be considered as an environmental assessment of the property.

5. The appraiser has based his or her appraisal report and valuation conclusion for an appraisal that is subject to satisfactory completion, repairs, or alterations on the assumption that the completion, repairs, or alterations of the subject property will be performed in a professional manner.

Appendixes

Exterior-Only Inspection Residential Appraisal Report   File

APPRAISER'S CERTIFICATION: The Appraiser certifies and agrees that:

1. I have, at a minimum, developed and reported this appraisal in accordance with the scope of work requirements stated in this appraisal report.

2. I performed a visual inspection of the exterior areas of the subject property from at least the street. I reported the condition of the improvements in factual, specific terms. I identified and reported the physical deficiencies that could affect the livability, soundness, or structural integrity of the property.

3. I performed this appraisal in accordance with the requirements of the Uniform Standards of Professional Appraisal Practice that were adopted and promulgated by the Appraisal Standards Board of The Appraisal Foundation and that were in place at the time this appraisal report was prepared.

4. I developed my opinion of the market value of the real property that is the subject of this report based on the sales comparison approach to value. I have adequate comparable market data to develop a reliable sales comparison approach for this appraisal assignment. I further certify that I considered the cost and income approaches to value but did not develop them, unless otherwise indicated in this report.

5. I researched, verified, analyzed, and reported on any current agreement for sale for the subject property, any offering for sale of the subject property in the twelve months prior to the effective date of this appraisal, and the prior sales of the subject property for a minimum of three years prior to the effective date of this appraisal, unless otherwise indicated in this report.

6. I researched, verified, analyzed, and reported on the prior sales of the comparable sales for a minimum of one year prior to the date of sale of the comparable sale, unless otherwise indicated in this report.

7. I selected and used comparable sales that are locationally, physically, and functionally the most similar to the subject property.

8. I have not used comparable sales that were the result of combining a land sale with the contract purchase price of a home that has been built or will be built on the land.

9. I have reported adjustments to the comparable sales that reflect the market's reaction to the differences between the subject property and the comparable sales.

10. I verified, from a disinterested source, all information in this report that was provided by parties who have a financial interest in the sale or financing of the subject property.

11. I have knowledge and experience in appraising this type of property in this market area.

12. I am aware of, and have access to, the necessary and appropriate public and private data sources, such as multiple listing services, tax assessment records, public land records and other such data sources for the area in which the property is located.

13. I obtained the information, estimates, and opinions furnished by other parties and expressed in this appraisal report from reliable sources that I believe to be true and correct.

14. I have taken into consideration the factors that have an impact on value with respect to the subject neighborhood, subject property, and the proximity of the subject property to adverse influences in the development of my opinion of market value. I have noted in this appraisal report any adverse conditions (such as, but not limited to, needed repairs, deterioration, the presence of hazardous wastes, toxic substances, adverse environmental conditions, etc.) observed during the inspection of the subject property or that I became aware of during the research involved in performing this appraisal. I have considered these adverse conditions in my analysis of the property value, and have reported on the effect of the conditions on the value and marketability of the subject property.

15. I have not knowingly withheld any significant information from this appraisal report and, to the best of my knowledge, all statements and information in this appraisal report are true and correct.

16. I stated in this appraisal report my own personal, unbiased, and professional analysis, opinions, and conclusions, which are subject only to the assumptions and limiting conditions in this appraisal report.

17. I have no present or prospective interest in the property that is the subject of this report, and I have no present or prospective personal interest or bias with respect to the participants in the transaction. I did not base, either partially or completely, my analysis and/or opinion of market value in this appraisal report on the race, color, religion, sex, age, marital status, handicap, familial status, or national origin of either the prospective owners or occupants of the subject property or of the present owners or occupants of the properties in the vicinity of the subject property or on any other basis prohibited by law.

18. My employment and/or compensation for performing this appraisal or any future or anticipated appraisals was not conditioned on any agreement or understanding, written or otherwise, that I would report (or present analysis supporting) a predetermined specific value, a predetermined minimum value, a range or direction in value, a value that favors the cause of any party, or the attainment of a specific result or occurrence of a specific subsequent event (such as approval of a pending mortgage loan application).

19. I personally prepared all conclusions and opinions about the real estate that were set forth in this appraisal report. If I relied on significant real property appraisal assistance from any individual or individuals in the performance of this appraisal or the preparation of this appraisal report, I have named such individual(s) and disclosed the specific tasks performed in this appraisal report. I certify that any individual so named is qualified to perform the tasks. I have not authorized anyone to make a change to any item in this appraisal report; therefore, any change made to this appraisal is unauthorized and I will take no responsibility for it.

Residential appraisal forms

Exterior-Only Inspection Residential Appraisal Report   File

20. I identified the lender/client in this appraisal report who is the individual, organization, or agent for the organization that ordered and will receive this appraisal report.

21. The lender/client may disclose or distribute this appraisal report to: the borrower; another lender at the request of the borrower; the mortgagee or its successors and assigns; mortgage insurers; government sponsored enterprises; other secondary market participants; data collection or reporting services; professional appraisal organizations; any department, agency, or instrumentality of the United States; and any state, the District of Columbia, or other jurisdictions; without having to obtain the appraiser's or supervisory appraiser's (if applicable) consent. Such consent must be obtained before this appraisal report may be disclosed or distributed to any other party (including, but not limited to, the public through advertising, public relations, news, sales, or other media).

22. I am aware that any disclosure or distribution of this appraisal report by me or the lender/client may be subject to certain laws and regulations. Further, I am also subject to the provisions of the Uniform Standards of Professional Appraisal Practice that pertain to disclosure or distribution by me.

23. The borrower, another lender at the request of the borrower, the mortgagee or its successors and assigns, mortgage insurers, government sponsored enterprises, and other secondary market participants may rely on this appraisal report as part of any mortgage finance transaction that involves any one or more of these parties.

24. If this appraisal report was transmitted as an "electronic record" containing my "electronic signature," as those terms are defined in applicable federal and/or state laws (excluding audio and video recordings), or a facsimile transmission of this appraisal report containing a copy or representation of my signature, the appraisal report shall be as effective, enforceable and valid as if a paper version of this appraisal report were delivered containing my original hand written signature.

25. Any intentional or negligent misrepresentation(s) contained in this appraisal report may result in civil liability and/or criminal penalties including, but not limited to, fine or imprisonment or both under the provisions of Title 18, United States Code, Section 1001, et seq., or similar state laws.

SUPERVISORY APPRAISER'S CERTIFICATION: The Supervisory Appraiser certifies and agrees that:

1. I directly supervised the appraiser for this appraisal assignment, have read the appraisal report, and agree with the appraiser's analysis, opinions, statements, conclusions, and the appraiser's certification.

2. I accept full responsibility for the contents of this appraisal report including, but not limited to, the appraiser's analysis, opinions, statements, conclusions, and the appraiser's certification.

3. The appraiser identified in this appraisal report is either a sub-contractor or an employee of the supervisory appraiser (or the appraisal firm), is qualified to perform this appraisal, and is acceptable to perform this appraisal under the applicable state law.

4. This appraisal report complies with the Uniform Standards of Professional Appraisal Practice that were adopted and promulgated by the Appraisal Standards Board of The Appraisal Foundation and that were in place at the time this appraisal report was prepared.

5. If this appraisal report was transmitted as an "electronic record" containing my "electronic signature," as those terms are defined in applicable federal and/or state laws (excluding audio and video recordings), or a facsimile transmission of this appraisal report containing a copy or representation of my signature, the appraisal report shall be as effective, enforceable and valid as if a paper version of this appraisal report were delivered containing my original hand written signature.

APPRAISER	SUPERVISORY APPRAISER (ONLY IF REQUIRED)
Signature _____	Signature _____
Name _____	Name _____
Company Name _____	Company Name _____
Company Address _____	Company Address _____
_____	_____
Telephone Number _____	Telephone Number _____
Email Address _____	Email Address _____
Date of Signature and Report _____	Date of Signature _____
Effective Date of Appraisal _____	State Certification # _____
State Certification # _____	or State License # _____
or State License # _____	State _____
or Other (describe) _____ State # _____	Expiration Date of Certification or License _____
State _____	
Expiration Date of Certification or License _____	SUBJECT PROPERTY
ADDRESS OF PROPERTY APPRAISED	☐ Did not inspect exterior of subject property
_____	☐ Did inspect exterior of subject property from street
_____	Date of Inspection _____
APPRAISED VALUE OF SUBJECT PROPERTY $ _____	
LENDER/CLIENT	COMPARABLE SALES
Name _____	☐ Did not inspect exterior of comparable sales from street
Company Name _____	☐ Did inspect exterior of comparable sales from street
Company Address _____	Date of Inspection _____
_____	
Email Address _____	

Appendixes

Manufactured Home Appraisal Report

File #

The purpose of this summary appraisal report is to provide the lender/client with an accurate, and adequately supported, opinion of the market value of the subject property.

SUBJECT

Property Address	City	State	Zip Code
Borrower	Owner of Public Record	County	
Legal Description			
Assessor's Parcel #	Tax Year	R.E. Taxes $	
Neighborhood Name	Map Reference	Census Tract	

Occupant ☐ Owner ☐ Tenant ☐ Vacant   Project Type (if applicable) ☐ PUD ☐ Condominium ☐ Cooperative ☐ Other (describe)

Special Assessments $ HOA $ ☐ per year ☐ per month

Property Rights Appraised ☐ Fee Simple ☐ Leasehold ☐ Other (describe)

Assignment Type ☐ Purchase Transaction ☐ Refinance Transaction ☐ Other (describe)

Lender/Client   Address

Is the subject property currently offered for sale or has it been offered for sale in the twelve months prior to the effective date of this appraisal? ☐ Yes ☐ No

Report data source(s) used, offering price(s), and date(s).

Manufactured homes located in either a condominium or cooperative project require the appraiser to inspect the project and complete the Project Information section of the Individual Condominium Unit Appraisal Report or the Individual Cooperative Interest Appraisal Report and attach it as an addendum to this report.

I ☐ did ☐ did not analyze the contract for sale for the subject purchase transaction. Explain the results of the analysis of the contract for sale or why the analysis was not performed.

CONTRACT

Contract Price $ Date of Contract   Is the property seller the owner of public record? ☐ Yes ☐ No Data Source(s)

Is there any financial assistance (loan charges, sale concessions, gift or downpayment assistance, etc.) to be paid by any party on behalf of the borrower? ☐ Yes ☐ No

If Yes, report the total dollar amount and describe the items to be paid.

I ☐ did ☐ did not analyze the manufacturer's invoice. Explain the results of the analysis of the manufacturer's invoice or why the analysis was not performed.

Retailer's Name (New Construction)

Note: Race and the racial composition of the neighborhood are not appraisal factors.

NEIGHBORHOOD

Neighborhood Characteristics			Manufactured Housing Trends			Manufactured Housing		Present Land Use %	
Location ☐ Urban ☐ Suburban ☐ Rural			Property Values ☐ Increasing ☐ Stable ☐ Declining			PRICE	AGE	One-Unit	%
Built-Up ☐ Over 75% ☐ 25–75% ☐ Under 25%			Demand/Supply ☐ Shortage ☐ In Balance ☐ Over Supply			$ (000)	(yrs)	2-4 Unit	%
Growth ☐ Rapid ☐ Stable ☐ Slow			Marketing Time ☐ Under 3 mths ☐ 3–6 mths ☐ Over 6 mths			Low		Multi-Family	%
Neighborhood Boundaries						High		Commercial	%
						Pred.		Other	%

Neighborhood Description

Market Conditions (including support for the above conclusions)

SITE

Dimensions	Area	Shape	View

Specific Zoning Classification   Zoning Description

Zoning Compliance ☐ Legal ☐ Legal Nonconforming (Grandfathered Use) ☐ No Zoning ☐ Illegal (describe)

Is the highest and best use of the subject property as improved (or as proposed per plans and specifications) the present use? ☐ Yes ☐ No If No, describe

Utilities	Public	Other (describe)		Public	Other (describe)	Off-site Improvements—Type	Public	Private
Electricity	☐	☐	Water	☐	☐	Street	☐	☐
Gas	☐	☐	Sanitary Sewer	☐	☐	Alley	☐	☐

FEMA Special Flood Hazard Area ☐ Yes ☐ No FEMA Flood Zone   FEMA Map #   FEMA Map Date

Are the utilities and off-site improvements typical for the market area? ☐ Yes ☐ No If No, describe

Is the site size, shape and topography generally conforming to and acceptable in the market area? ☐ Yes ☐ No If No, explain

Is there adequate vehicular access to the subject property? ☐ Yes ☐ No If No, describe

Is the street properly maintained? ☐ Yes ☐ No If No, describe

Are there any adverse site conditions or external factors (easements, encroachments, environmental conditions, land uses, etc.)? ☐ Yes ☐ No If Yes, describe

HUD DATA PLATE

The HUD Data Plate/Compliance Certificate is located on the interior of the subject and contains, among other things, the manufacturer's name, trade/model name, year manufactured and serial number. The HUD Certification Label is located on the exterior of each section of the home.

Is the HUD Data Plate/Compliance Certificate attached to the dwelling? ☐ Yes ☐ No If Yes, identify the location. If No, provide the data source(s) for the HUD Data Plate/Compliance Certificate information.

Is a HUD Certification Label attached to the exterior of each section of the dwelling? ☐ Yes ☐ No If No, provide the data source(s) for the HUD Certification Label #'s

Manufacturer's Serial #(s)/VIN #(s)

HUD Certification Label #(s)

Manufacturer's Name   Trade/Model   Date of Manufacture

Do the Wind, Roof Load, and Thermal Zones meet the minimum HUD requirements for the location of the subject property? ☐ Yes ☐ No If No, explain

Manufactured Home Appraisal Report

File #

General Description	Foundation	Exterior Description materials/condition	Interior materials/condition
# of Units ☐ One ☐ Additions	☐ Poured Concrete ☐ Concrete Runners	Skirting	Floors
# of Stories ☐ 1 ☐ 2 ☐ Other	☐ Block & Pier ☐ Other-att. description	Exterior Walls	Walls
Design (Style)	☐ Full Basement ☐ Partial Basement	Roof Surface	Trim/Finish
# of Sections ☐ 1 ☐ 2 ☐ 3	Basement Area sq. ft.	Gutters & Downspouts	Bath Floor
☐ Other	Basement Finish %	Window Type	Bath Wainscot
Type ☐ Det. ☐ Att. ☐ S-Det./End Unit	☐ Outside Entry/Exit ☐ Sump Pump	Storm Sash/Insulated	Car Storage ☐ None
☐ Existing ☐ Proposed ☐ Under Const.	Evidence of ☐ Infestation	Screens	☐ Driveway # of Cars
Year Built Effective Age (Yrs)	☐ Dampness ☐ Settlement	Doors	Driveway Surface
Attic ☐ None	Heating ☐ FWA ☐ HWBB ☐ Radiant	Amenities ☐ WoodStove(s) #	☐ Garage # of Cars
☐ Drop Stair ☐ Stairs	☐ Other Fuel	☐ Fireplace(s) # ☐ Fence	☐ Carport # of Cars
☐ Floor ☐ Scuttle	Cooling ☐ Central Air Conditioning	☐ Patio/Deck ☐ Porch	☐ Attached ☐ Detached
☐ Finished ☐ Heated	☐ Individual ☐ Other	☐ Pool ☐ Other	☐ Built-in

Appliances ☐ Refrigerator ☐ Range/Oven ☐ Dishwasher ☐ Disposal ☐ Microwave ☐ Washer/Dryer ☐ Other (describe)

Finished area **above** grade contains: Rooms Bedrooms Bath(s) Square Feet of Gross Living Area Above Grade

Describe any additions or modifications (decks, rooms, remodeling, etc.)

Installer's Name Date Installed Model Year

Is the manufactured home attached to a permanent foundation system? ☐ Yes ☐ No If No, describe the foundation sytem and the manner of attachment.

Have the towing hitch, wheels, and axles been removed? ☐ Yes ☐ No If No, explain

Is the manufactured home permanently connected to a septic tank or sewage system and other utilities? ☐ Yes ☐ No If No, explain

Does the dwelling have sufficient gross living area and room dimensions to be acceptable to the market? ☐ Yes ☐ No If No, explain

Additional features (special energy efficient items, non-realty items, etc.)

The appraiser must rate the quality of construction for the subject unit based on objective criteria (such as N.A.D.A. Manufactured Housing Appraisal Guide®, Marshall & Swift Residential Cost Handbook®, or other published cost service). The appraiser must also report the source used for this quality of construction rating determination.
Quality ☐ Poor ☐ Fair ☐ Average ☐ Good ☐ Excellent Identify source of quality rating

Describe the condition of the property (including needed repairs, deterioration, renovations, remodeling, etc.).

Are there any physical deficiencies or adverse conditions that affect the livability, soundness, or structural integrity of the property? ☐ Yes ☐ No If Yes, describe

Does the property generally conform to the neighborhood (functional utility, style, condition, use, construction, etc.)? ☐ Yes ☐ No If No, describe

Provide adequate information for the lender/client to replicate the below cost figures and calculations.

Support for the opinion of site value (summary of comparable land sales or other methods for estimating site value)

ESTIMATED ☐ REPRODUCTION OR ☐ REPLACEMENT COST NEW

Source of cost data	Effective date of cost data	Quality rating from cost service	
OPINION OF SITE VALUE	$	**Exterior Dimensions of the Subject Unit**	
Section One Sq. ft. @ $	$	X =	Sq. ft.
Section Two Sq. ft. @ $	$	X =	Sq. ft.
Section Three Sq. ft. @ $	$	X =	Sq. ft.
Section Four Sq. ft. @ $	$	X =	Sq. ft.
	$	Total Gross Living Area:	Sq. ft.
	$	**Other Data Identification**	
		N.A.D.A. Data Identification Info: Edition Mo: Yr:	
Sub-total: $		MH State: Region: Size: ft. x ft.	
Cost Multiplier (if applicable): x		Gray pg. White pg. Black SVS pg.	
Modified Sub-total:		15 years and older Conversion Chart pg. Yellow pg.	
Physical Depreciation or Condition Modifier:		Comments	
Functional Obsolescence (not used for N.A.D.A.):			
External Depreciation or State Location Modifier:			
Delivery, Installation, and Setup (not used for N.A.D.A.): $			
Other Depreciated Site Improvements: $			
Market Value of Subject Site (as supported above): $			
Indicated Value by Cost Approach: $		Estimated Remaining Economic Life (HUD and VA only) Years	

Summary of Cost Approach

Manufactured Home Appraisal Report

File #

There are comparable properties currently offered for sale in the subject neighborhood ranging in price from $ to $.

There are comparable sales in the subject neighborhood within the past twelve months ranging in sale price from $ to $.

SALES COMPARISON APPROACH

FEATURE	SUBJECT	COMPARABLE SALE # 1		COMPARABLE SALE # 2		COMPARABLE SALE # 3	
Address							
Proximity to Subject							
Sale Price	$		$		$		$
Sale Price/Gross Liv. Area	$ sq. ft.	$ sq. ft.		$ sq. ft.		$ sq. ft.	
Manufactured Home		☐ Yes ☐ No		☐ Yes ☐ No		☐ Yes ☐ No	
Data Source(s)							
Verification Source(s)							
VALUE ADJUSTMENTS	DESCRIPTION	DESCRIPTION	+(-) $ Adjustment	DESCRIPTION	+(-) $ Adjustment	DESCRIPTION	+(-) $ Adjustment
Sale or Financing Concessions							
Date of Sale/Time							
Location							
Leasehold/Fee Simple							
Site							
View							
Design (Style)							
Quality of Construction							
Actual Age							
Condition							
Above Grade Room Count	Total Bdrms. Baths	Total Bdrms. Baths		Total Bdrms. Baths		Total Bdrms. Baths	
Gross Living Area	sq. ft.	sq. ft.		sq. ft.		sq. ft.	
Basement & Finished Rooms Below Grade							
Functional Utility							
Heating/Cooling							
Energy Efficient Items							
Garage/Carport							
Porch/Patio/Deck							
Net Adjustment (Total)		☐ + ☐ -	$	☐ + ☐ -	$	☐ + ☐ -	$
Adjusted Sale Price of Comparables		Net Adj. % Gross Adj. %	$	Net Adj. % Gross Adj. %	$	Net Adj. % Gross Adj. %	$

I ☐ did ☐ did not research the sale or transfer history of the subject property and comparable sales. If not, explain

My research ☐ did ☐ did not reveal any prior sales or transfers of the subject property for the three years prior to the effective date of this appraisal.

Data source(s)

My research ☐ did ☐ did not reveal any prior sales or transfers of the comparable sales for the year prior to the date of sale of the comparable sale.

Data source(s)

Report the results of the research and analysis of the prior sale or transfer history of the subject property and comparable sales (report additional prior sales on page 4).

ITEM	SUBJECT	COMPARABLE SALE # 1	COMPARABLE SALE # 2	COMPARABLE SALE # 3
Date of Prior Sale/Transfer				
Price of Prior Sale/Transfer				
Data Source(s)				
Effective Date of Data Source(s)				

Analysis of prior sale or transfer history of the subject property and comparable sales

Summary of Sales Comparison Approach

Indicated Value by Sales Comparison Approach $

RECONCILIATION

Indicated Value by: Sales Comparison Approach $ Cost Approach $ Income Approach (if developed) $

This appraisal is made ☐ "as is", ☐ subject to completion per plans and specifications on the basis of a hypothetical condition that the improvements have been completed, ☐ subject to the following repairs or alterations on the basis of a hypothetical condition that the repairs or alterations have been completed, or ☐ subject to the following required inspection based on the extraordinary assumption that the condition or deficiency does not require alteration or repair.

Based on a complete visual inspection of the interior and exterior areas of the subject property, defined scope of work, statement of assumptions and limiting conditions, and appraiser's certification, my (our) opinion of the market value, as defined, of the real property that is the subject of this report is $, as of , which is the date of inspection and the effective date of this appraisal.

Freddie Mac Form 70B March 2005 Page 3 of 7 Fannie Mae Form 1004C March 2005

Manufactured Home Appraisal Report

File #

ADDITIONAL COMMENTS

INCOME APPROACH TO VALUE (not required by Fannie Mae.)

Estimated Monthly Market Rent $ _____ X Gross Rent Multiplier _____ = $ _____ Indicated Value by Income Approach

Summary of Income Approach (including support for market rent and GRM)

PROJECT INFORMATION FOR PUDs (if applicable)

Is the developer/builder in control of the Homeowners' Association (HOA)? ☐ Yes ☐ No   Unit type(s) ☐ Detached ☐ Attached

Provide the following information for PUDs ONLY if the developer/builder is in control of the HOA and the subject property is an attached dwelling unit.

Legal name of project

Total number of phases	Total number of units	Total number of units sold
Total number of units rented	Total number of units for sale	Data source(s)

Was the project created by the conversion of existing building(s) into a PUD? ☐ Yes ☐ No If Yes, date of conversion

Does the project contain any multi-dwelling units? ☐ Yes ☐ No Data source(s)

Are the units, common elements, and recreation facilities complete? ☐ Yes ☐ No If No, describe the status of completion.

Are the common elements leased to or by the Homeowners' Association? ☐ Yes ☐ No If Yes, describe the rental terms and options.

Describe common elements and recreational facilities.

Manufactured Home Appraisal Report

This report form is designed to report an appraisal of a one-unit manufactured home; including a manufactured home in a planned unit development (PUD). A Manufactured home located in either a condominium or cooperative project requires the appraiser to inspect the project and complete the project information section of the Individual Condominium Unit Appraisal Report or the Individual Cooperative Interest Appraisal Report and attach it as an addendum to this report.

This appraisal report is subject to the following scope of work, intended use, intended user, definition of market value, statement of assumptions and limiting conditions, and certifications. Modifications, additions, or deletions to the intended use, intended user, definition of market value, or assumptions and limiting conditions are not permitted. The appraiser may expand the scope of work to include any additional research or analysis necessary based on the complexity of this appraisal assignment. Modifications or deletions to the certifications are also not permitted. However, additional certifications that do not constitute material alterations to this appraisal report, such as those required by law or those related to the appraiser's continuing education or membership in an appraisal organization, are permitted.

SCOPE OF WORK: The scope of work for this appraisal is defined by the complexity of this appraisal assignment and the reporting requirements of this appraisal report form, including the following definition of market value, statement of assumptions and limiting conditions, and certifications. The appraiser must, at a minimum: (1) perform a complete visual inspection of the interior and exterior areas of the subject property, (2) inspect the neighborhood, (3) inspect each of the comparable sales from at least the street, (4) research, verify, and analyze data from reliable public and/or private sources, and (5) report his or her analysis, opinions, and conclusions in this appraisal report.

INTENDED USE: The intended use of this appraisal report is for the lender/client to evaluate the property that is the subject of this appraisal for a mortgage finance transaction.

INTENDED USER: The intended user of this appraisal report is the lender/client.

DEFINITION OF MARKET VALUE: The most probable price which a property should bring in a competitive and open market under all conditions requisite to a fair sale, the buyer and seller, each acting prudently, knowledgeably and assuming the price is not affected by undue stimulus. Implicit in this definition is the consummation of a sale as of a specified date and the passing of title from seller to buyer under conditions whereby: (1) buyer and seller are typically motivated; (2) both parties are well informed or well advised, and each acting in what he or she considers his or her own best interest; (3) a reasonable time is allowed for exposure in the open market; (4) payment is made in terms of cash in U. S. dollars or in terms of financial arrangements comparable thereto; and (5) the price represents the normal consideration for the property sold unaffected by special or creative financing or sales concessions* granted by anyone associated with the sale.

*Adjustments to the comparables must be made for special or creative financing or sales concessions. No adjustments are necessary for those costs which are normally paid by sellers as a result of tradition or law in a market area; these costs are readily identifiable since the seller pays these costs in virtually all sales transactions. Special or creative financing adjustments can be made to the comparable property by comparisons to financing terms offered by a third party institutional lender that is not already involved in the property or transaction. Any adjustment should not be calculated on a mechanical dollar for dollar cost of the financing or concession but the dollar amount of any adjustment should approximate the market's reaction to the financing or concessions based on the appraiser's judgment.

STATEMENT OF ASSUMPTIONS AND LIMITING CONDITIONS: The appraiser's certification in this report is subject to the following assumptions and limiting conditions:

1. The appraiser will not be responsible for matters of a legal nature that affect either the property being appraised or the title to it, except for information that he or she became aware of during the research involved in performing this appraisal. The appraiser assumes that the title is good and marketable and will not render any opinions about the title.

2. The appraiser has provided a sketch in this appraisal report to show approximate dimensions of the improvements. The sketch is included only to assist the reader in visualizing the property and understanding the appraiser's determination of its size.

3. The appraiser has examined the available flood maps that are provided by the Federal Emergency Management Agency (or other data sources) and has noted in this appraisal report whether any portion of the subject site is located in an identified Special Flood Hazard Area. Because the appraiser is not a surveyor, he or she makes no guarantees, express or implied, regarding this determination.

4. The appraiser will not give testimony or appear in court because he or she made an appraisal of the property in question, unless specific arrangements to do so have been made beforehand, or as otherwise required by law.

5. The appraiser has noted in this appraisal report any adverse conditions (such as needed repairs, deterioration, the presence of hazardous wastes, toxic substances, etc.) observed during the inspection of the subject property or that he or she became aware of during the research involved in performing this appraisal. Unless otherwise stated in this appraisal report, the appraiser has no knowledge of any hidden or unapparent physical deficiencies or adverse conditions of the property (such as, but not limited to, needed repairs, deterioration, the presence of hazardous wastes, toxic substances, adverse environmental conditions, etc.) that would make the property less valuable, and has assumed that there are no such conditions and makes no guarantees or warranties, express or implied. The appraiser will not be responsible for any such conditions that do exist or for any engineering or testing that might be required to discover whether such conditions exist. Because the appraiser is not an expert in the field of environmental hazards, this appraisal report must not be considered as an environmental assessment of the property.

6. The appraiser has based his or her appraisal report and valuation conclusion for an appraisal that is subject to satisfactory completion, repairs, or alterations on the assumption that the completion, repairs, or alterations of the subject property will be performed in a professional manner.

Residential appraisal forms

Manufactured Home Appraisal Report   File

APPRAISER'S CERTIFICATION: The Appraiser certifies and agrees that:

1. I have, at a minimum, developed and reported this appraisal in accordance with the scope of work requirements stated in this appraisal report.

2. I performed a complete visual inspection of the interior and exterior areas of the subject property. I reported the condition of the improvements in factual, specific terms. I identified and reported the physical deficiencies that could affect the livability, soundness, or structural integrity of the property.

3. I performed this appraisal in accordance with the requirements of the Uniform Standards of Professional Appraisal Practice that were adopted and promulgated by the Appraisal Standards Board of The Appraisal Foundation and that were in place at the time this appraisal report was prepared.

4. I developed my opinion of the market value of the real property that is the subject of this report based on the sales comparison approach to value. I also developed the cost approach to value as support for the sales comparison approach. I have adequate comparable market and cost data to develop reliable sales comparison and cost approaches for this appraisal assignment. I further certify that I considered the income approach to value but did not develop it, unless otherwise indicated in this report.

5. I researched, verified, analyzed, and reported on any current agreement for sale for the subject property, any offering for sale of the subject property in the twelve months prior to the effective date of this appraisal, and the prior sales of the subject property for a minimum of three years prior to the effective date of this appraisal, unless otherwise indicated in this report.

6. I researched, verified, analyzed, and reported on the prior sales of the comparable sales for a minimum of one year prior to the date of sale of the comparable sale, unless otherwise indicated in this report.

7. I selected and used comparable sales that are locationally, physically, and functionally the most similar to the subject property.

8. I have not used comparable sales that were the result of combining a land sale with the contract purchase price of a home that has been built or will be built on the land.

9. I have reported adjustments to the comparable sales that reflect the market's reaction to the differences between the subject property and the comparable sales.

10. I verified, from a disinterested source, all information in this report that was provided by parties who have a financial interest in the sale or financing of the subject property.

11. I have knowledge and experience in appraising this type of property in this market area.

12. I am aware of, and have access to, the necessary and appropriate public and private data sources, such as multiple listing services, tax assessment records, public land records and other such data sources for the area in which the property is located.

13. I obtained the information, estimates, and opinions furnished by other parties and expressed in this appraisal report from reliable sources that I believe to be true and correct.

14. I have taken into consideration the factors that have an impact on value with respect to the subject neighborhood, subject property, and the proximity of the subject property to adverse influences in the development of my opinion of market value. I have noted in this appraisal report any adverse conditions (such as, but not limited to, needed repairs, deterioration, the presence of hazardous wastes, toxic substances, adverse environmental conditions, etc.) observed during the inspection of the subject property or that I became aware of during the research involved in performing this appraisal. I have considered these adverse conditions in my analysis of the property value, and have reported on the effect of the conditions on the value and marketability of the subject property.

15. I have not knowingly withheld any significant information from this appraisal report and, to the best of my knowledge, all statements and information in this appraisal report are true and correct.

16. I stated in this appraisal report my own personal, unbiased, and professional analysis, opinions, and conclusions, which are subject only to the assumptions and limiting conditions in this appraisal report.

17. I have no present or prospective interest in the property that is the subject of this report, and I have no present or prospective personal interest or bias with respect to the participants in the transaction. I did not base, either partially or completely, my analysis and/or opinion of market value in this appraisal report on the race, color, religion, sex, age, marital status, handicap, familial status, or national origin of either the prospective owners or occupants of the subject property or of the present owners or occupants of the properties in the vicinity of the subject property or on any other basis prohibited by law.

18. My employment and/or compensation for performing this appraisal or any future or anticipated appraisals was not conditioned on any agreement or understanding, written or otherwise, that I would report (or present analysis supporting) a predetermined specific value, a predetermined minimum value, a range or direction in value, a value that favors the cause of any party, or the attainment of a specific result or occurrence of a specific subsequent event (such as approval of a pending mortgage loan application).

19. I personally prepared all conclusions and opinions about the real estate that were set forth in this appraisal report. If I relied on significant real property appraisal assistance from any individual or individuals in the performance of this appraisal or the preparation of this appraisal report, I have named such individual(s) and disclosed the specific tasks performed in this appraisal report. I certify that any individual so named is qualified to perform the tasks. I have not authorized anyone to make a change to any item in this appraisal report; therefore, any change made to this appraisal is unauthorized and I will take no responsibility for it.

20. I identified the lender/client in this appraisal report who is the individual, organization, or agent for the organization that ordered and will receive this appraisal report.

Manufactured Home Appraisal Report
File #

21. The lender/client may disclose or distribute this appraisal report to: the borrower; another lender at the request of the borrower; the mortgagee or its successors and assigns; mortgage insurers; government sponsored enterprises; other secondary market participants; data collection or reporting services; professional appraisal organizations; any department, agency, or instrumentality of the United States; and any state, the District of Columbia, or other jurisdictions; without having to obtain the appraiser's or supervisory appraiser's (if applicable) consent. Such consent must be obtained before this appraisal report may be disclosed or distributed to any other party (including, but not limited to, the public through advertising, public relations, news, sales, or other media).

22. I am aware that any disclosure or distribution of this appraisal report by me or the lender/client may be subject to certain laws and regulations. Further, I am also subject to the provisions of the Uniform Standards of Professional Appraisal Practice that pertain to disclosure or distribution by me.

23. The borrower, another lender at the request of the borrower, the mortgagee or its successors and assigns, mortgage insurers, government sponsored enterprises, and other secondary market participants may rely on this appraisal report as part of any mortgage finance transaction that involves any one or more of these parties.

24. If this appraisal report was transmitted as an "electronic record" containing my "electronic signature," as those terms are defined in applicable federal and/or state laws (excluding audio and video recordings), or a facsimile transmission of this appraisal report containing a copy or representation of my signature, the appraisal report shall be as effective, enforceable and valid as if a paper version of this appraisal report were delivered containing my original hand written signature.

25. Any intentional or negligent misrepresentation(s) contained in this appraisal report may result in civil liability and/or criminal penalties including, but not limited to, fine or imprisonment or both under the provisions of Title 18, United States Code, Section 1001, et seq., or similar state laws.

SUPERVISORY APPRAISER'S CERTIFICATION: The Supervisory Appraiser certifies and agrees that:

1. I directly supervised the appraiser for this appraisal assignment, have read the appraisal report, and agree with the appraiser's analysis, opinions, statements, conclusions, and the appraiser's certification.

2. I accept full responsibility for the contents of this appraisal report including, but not limited to, the appraiser's analysis, opinions, statements, conclusions, and the appraiser's certification.

3. The appraiser identified in this appraisal report is either a sub-contractor or an employee of the supervisory appraiser (or the appraisal firm), is qualified to perform this appraisal, and is acceptable to perform this appraisal under the applicable state law.

4. This appraisal report complies with the Uniform Standards of Professional Appraisal Practice that were adopted and promulgated by the Appraisal Standards Board of The Appraisal Foundation and that were in place at the time this appraisal report was prepared.

5. If this appraisal report was transmitted as an "electronic record" containing my "electronic signature," as those terms are defined in applicable federal and/or state laws (excluding audio and video recordings), or a facsimile transmission of this appraisal report containing a copy or representation of my signature, the appraisal report shall be as effective, enforceable and valid as if a paper version of this appraisal report were delivered containing my original hand written signature.

APPRAISER

Signature _____
Name_____
Company Name_____
Company Address _____
_____
Telephone Number _____
Email Address _____
Date of Signature and Report _____
Effective Date of Appraisal _____
State Certification # _____
or State License # _____
or Other _____
State _____
Expiration Date of Certification or License _____

ADDRESS OF PROPERTY APPRAISED

_____
_____
APPRAISED VALUE OF SUBJECT PROPERTY $ _____

LENDER/CLIENT

Name_____
Company Name_____
Company Address _____
Email Address _____

SUPERVISORY APPRAISER (ONLY IF REQUIRED)

Signature _____
Name_____
Company Name_____
Company Address _____
_____
Telephone Number _____
Email Address _____
Date Signature_____
State Certification # _____
or State License # _____
State_____
Expiration Date of Certification or License _____

SUBJECT PROPERTY

☐ Did not inspect subject property
☐ Did inspect exterior of subject property from street
   Date of Inspection_____
☐ Did inspect interior and exterior of subject property
   Date of Inspection_____

COMPARABLE SALES

☐ Did not inspect exterior of comparable sales from street
☐ Did inspect exterior of comparable sales from street
   Date of Inspection_____

Residential appraisal forms

Individual Condominium Unit Appraisal Report

File #

The purpose of this summary appraisal report is to provide the lender/client with an accurate, and adequately supported, opinion of the market value of the subject property.

SUBJECT

| Property Address | Unit # | City | State | Zip Code |

Borrower   Owner of Public Record   County

Legal Description

Assessor's Parcel #   Tax Year   R.E. Taxes $

Project Name   Phase #   Map Reference   Census Tract

Occupant ☐ Owner ☐ Tenant ☐ Vacant   Special Assessments $ HOA $ ☐ per year ☐ per month

Property Rights Appraised ☐ Fee Simple ☐ Leasehold ☐ Other (describe)

Assignment Type ☐ Purchase Transaction ☐ Refinance Transaction ☐ Other (describe)

Lender/Client   Address

Is the subject property currently offered for sale or has it been offered for sale in the twelve months prior to the effective date of this appraisal? ☐ Yes ☐ No

Report data source(s) used, offering price(s), and date(s).

CONTRACT

I ☐ did ☐ did not analyze the contract for sale for the subject purchase transaction. Explain the results of the analysis of the contract for sale or why the analysis was not performed.

Contract Price $ Date of Contract   Is the property seller the owner of public record? ☐ Yes ☐ No   Data Source(s)

Is there any financial assistance (loan charges, sale concessions, gift or downpayment assistance, etc.) to be paid by any party on behalf of the borrower? ☐ Yes ☐ No
If Yes, report the total dollar amount and describe the items to be paid.

NEIGHBORHOOD

Note: Race and the racial composition of the neighborhood are not appraisal factors.

Neighborhood Characteristics			Condominium Unit Housing Trends				Condominium Housing		Present Land Use %	
Location ☐ Urban	☐ Suburban	☐ Rural	Property Values ☐ Increasing	☐ Stable	☐ Declining		PRICE	AGE	One-Unit	%
Built-Up ☐ Over 75%	☐ 25–75%	☐ Under 25%	Demand/Supply ☐ Shortage	☐ In Balance	☐ Over Supply		$ (000)	(yrs)	2-4 Unit	%
Growth ☐ Rapid	☐ Stable	☐ Slow	Marketing Time ☐ Under 3 mths	☐ 3–6 mths	☐ Over 6 mths		Low		Multi-Family	%
Neighborhood Boundaries							High		Commercial	%
							Pred.		Other	%

Neighborhood Description

Market Conditions (including support for the above conclusions)

PROJECT SITE

| Topography | | Size | | Density | | View | |

Specific Zoning Classification   Zoning Description

Zoning Compliance ☐ Legal ☐ Legal Nonconforming – Do the zoning regulations permit rebuilding to current density? ☐ Yes ☐ No
☐ No Zoning ☐ Illegal (describe)

Is the highest and best use of the subject property as improved (or as proposed per plans and specifications) the present use? ☐ Yes ☐ No If No, describe

Utilities	Public	Other (describe)		Public	Other (describe)	Off-site Improvements—Type	Public	Private
Electricity	☐	☐	Water	☐	☐	Street	☐	☐
Gas	☐	☐	Sanitary Sewer	☐	☐	Alley	☐	☐

FEMA Special Flood Hazard Area ☐ Yes ☐ No   FEMA Flood Zone   FEMA Map #   FEMA Map Date

Are the utilities and off-site improvements typical for the market area? ☐ Yes ☐ No If No, describe

Are there any adverse site conditions or external factors (easements, encroachments, environmental conditions, land uses, etc.)? ☐ Yes ☐ No If Yes, describe

PROJECT INFORMATION

Data source(s) for project information

Project Description ☐ Detached ☐ Row or Townhouse ☐ Garden ☐ Mid-Rise ☐ High-Rise ☐ Other (describe)

General Description	General Description	Subject Phase	If Project Completed	If Project Incomplete
# of Stories	Exterior Walls	# of Units	# of Phases	# of Planned Phases
# of Elevators	Roof Surface	# of Units Completed	# of Units	# o f Planned Units
☐ Existing ☐ Proposed	Total # Parking	# of Units For Sale	# of Units for Sale	# of Units for Sale
☐ Under Construction	Ratio (spaces/units)	# of Units Sold	# of Units Sold	# of Units Sold
Year Built	Type	# of Units Rented	# of Units Rented	# of Units Rented
Effective Age	Guest Parking	# of Owner Occupied Units	# of Owner Occupied Units	# of Owner Occupied Units

Project Primary Occupancy ☐ Principle Residence ☐ Second Home or Recreational ☐ Tenant

Is the developer/builder in control of the Homeowners' Association (HOA)? ☐ Yes ☐ No

Management Group – ☐ Homeowners' Association ☐ Developer ☐ Management Agent – Provide name of management company.

Does any single entity (the same individual, investor group, corporation, etc.) own more than 10% of the total units in the project? ☐ Yes ☐ No If Yes, describe

Was the project created by the conversion of an existing building(s) into a condominium? ☐ Yes ☐ No If Yes, describe the original use and the date of conversion.

Are the units, common elements, and recreation facilities complete (including any planned rehabilitation for a condominium conversion)? ☐ Yes ☐ No If No, describe

Is there any commercial space in the project? ☐ Yes ☐ No If Yes, describe and indicate the overall percentage of the commercial space.

Appendixes

Individual Condominium Unit Appraisal Report

File #

PROJECT INFORMATION

Describe the condition of the project and quality of construction.

Describe the common elements and recreational facilities.

Are any common elements leased to or by the Homeowners' Association? ☐ Yes ☐ No If Yes, describe the rental terms and options.

Is the project subject to ground rent? ☐ Yes ☐ No If Yes, $ _____ per year (describe terms and conditions)

Are the parking facilities adequate for the project size and type? ☐ Yes ☐ No If No, describe and comment on the effect on value and marketability.

PROJECT ANALYSIS

I ☐ did ☐ did not analyze the condominium project budget for the current year. Explain the results of the analysis of the budget (adequacy of fees, reserves, etc.), or why the analysis was not performed.

Are there any other fees (other than regular HOA charges) for the use of the project facilities? ☐ Yes ☐ No If Yes, report the charges and describe.

Compared to other competitive projects of similar quality and design, the subject unit charge appears ☐ High ☐ Average ☐ Low If High or Low, describe

Are there any special or unusual characteristics of the project (based on the condominium documents, HOA meetings, or other information) known to the appraiser? ☐ Yes ☐ No If Yes, describe and explain the effect on value and marketability.

Unit Charge $ _____ per month X 12 = $ _____ per year   Annual assessment charge per year per square feet of gross living area = $ _____

Utilities included in the unit monthly assessment ☐ None ☐ Heat ☐ Air Conditioning ☐ Electricity ☐ Gas ☐ Water ☐ Sewer ☐ Cable ☐ Other (describe)

UNIT DESCRIPTION

General Description	Interior materials/condition	Amenities	Appliances	Car Storage
Floor #	Floors	☐ Fireplace(s) #	☐ Refrigerator	☐ None
# of Levels	Walls	☐ Woodstove(s) #	☐ Range/Oven	☐ Garage ☐ Covered ☐ Open
Heating Type Fuel	Trim/Finish	☐ Deck/Patio	☐ Disp ☐ Microwave	# of Cars
☐ Central AC ☐ Individual AC	Bath Wainscot	☐ Porch/Balcony	☐ Dishwasher	☐ Assigned ☐ Owned
☐ Other (describe)	Doors	☐ Other	☐ Washer/Dryer	Parking Space #

Finished area **above** grade contains: Rooms   Bedrooms   Bath(s)   Square Feet of Gross Living Area Above Grade

Are the heating and cooling for the individual units separately metered? ☐ Yes ☐ No If No, describe and comment on compatibility to other projects in the market area.

Additional features (special energy efficient items, etc.)

Describe the condition of the property (including needed repairs, deterioration, renovations, remodeling, etc.).

Are there any physical deficiencies or adverse conditions that affect the livability, soundness, or structural integrity of the property? ☐ Yes ☐ No If Yes, describe

Does the property generally conform to the neighborhood (functional utility, style, condition, use, construction, etc.)? ☐ Yes ☐ No If No, describe

PRIOR SALE HISTORY

I ☐ did ☐ did not research the sale or transfer history of the subject property and comparable sales. If not, explain

My research ☐ did ☐ did not reveal any prior sales or transfers of the subject property for the three years prior to the effective date of this appraisal.

Data source(s)

My research ☐ did ☐ did not reveal any prior sales or transfers of the comparable sales for the year prior to the date of sale of the comparable sale.

Data source(s)

Report the results of the research and analysis of the prior sale or transfer history of the subject property and comparable sales (report additional prior sales on page 3).

ITEM	SUBJECT	COMPARABLE SALE # 1	COMPARABLE SALE # 2	COMPARABLE SALE # 3
Date of Prior Sale/Transfer				
Price of Prior Sale/Transfer				
Data Source(s)				
Effective Date of Data Source(s)				

Analysis of prior sale or transfer history of the subject property and comparable sales.

Freddie Mac Form 465   March 2005   Page 2 of 6   Fannie Mae Form 1073   March 2005

Residential appraisal forms

Individual Condominium Unit Appraisal Report

File #

There are	comparable properties currently offered for sale in the subject neighborhood ranging in price from $		to $	.
There are	comparable sales in the subject neighborhood within the past twelve months ranging in sale price from $		to $	.

FEATURE	SUBJECT	COMPARABLE SALE # 1		COMPARABLE SALE # 2		COMPARABLE SALE # 3	
Address and Unit #							
Project Name and Phase							
Proximity to Subject							
Sale Price	$		$		$		$
Sale Price/Gross Liv. Area	$ sq. ft.	$ sq. ft.		$ sq. ft.		$ sq. ft.	
Data Source(s)							
Verification Source(s)							
VALUE ADJUSTMENTS	DESCRIPTION	DESCRIPTION	+(-) $ Adjustment	DESCRIPTION	+(-) $ Adjustment	DESCRIPTION	+(-) $ Adjustment
Sale or Financing Concessions							
Date of Sale/Time							
Location							
Leasehold/Fee Simple							
HOA Mo. Assessment							
Common Elements and Rec. Facilities							
Floor Location							
View							
Design (Style)							
Quality of Construction							
Actual Age							
Condition							
Above Grade	Total	Bdrms.	Baths	Total	Bdrms.	Baths	Total	Bdrms.	Baths	Total	Bdrms.	Baths
Room Count							
Gross Living Area	sq. ft.	sq. ft.		sq. ft.		sq. ft.	
Basement & Finished Rooms Below Grade							
Functional Utility							
Heating/Cooling							
Energy Efficient Items							
Garage/Carport							
Porch/Patio/Deck							
Net Adjustment (Total)		☐ + ☐ -	$	☐ + ☐ -	$	☐ + ☐ -	$
Adjusted Sale Price of Comparables		Net Adj. % Gross Adj. %	$	Net Adj. % Gross Adj. %	$	Net Adj. % Gross Adj. %	$

Summary of Sales Comparison Approach

Indicated Value by Sales Comparison Approach $

INCOME APPROACH TO VALUE (not required by Fannie Mae)		
Estimated Monthly Market Rent $ X Gross Rent Multiplier = $ Indicated Value by Income Approach		

Summary of Income Approach (including support for market rent and GRM)

Indicated Value by: Sales Comparison Approach $ Income Approach (if developed) $

This appraisal is made ☐ "as is", ☐ subject to completion per plans and specifications on the basis of a hypothetical condition that the improvements have been completed, ☐ subject to the following repairs or alterations on the basis of a hypothetical condition that the repairs or alterations have been completed, or ☐ subject to the following required inspection based on the extraordinary assumption that the condition or deficiency does not require alteration or repair:

Based on a complete visual inspection of the interior and exterior areas of the subject property, defined scope of work, statement of assumptions and limiting conditions, and appraiser's certification, my (our) opinion of the market value, as defined, of the real property that is the subject of this report is $, as of   , which is the date of inspection and the effective date of this appraisal.

Appendixes

Individual Condominium Unit Appraisal Report

This report form is designed to report an appraisal of a unit in a condominium project or a condominium unit in a planned unit development (PUD). This report form is not designed to report an appraisal of a manufactured home or a unit in a cooperative project.

This appraisal report is subject to the following scope of work, intended use, intended user, definition of market value, statement of assumptions and limiting conditions, and certifications. Modifications, additions, or deletions to the intended use, intended user, definition of market value, or assumptions and limiting conditions are not permitted. The appraiser may expand the scope of work to include any additional research or analysis necessary based on the complexity of this appraisal assignment. Modifications or deletions to the certifications are also not permitted. However, additional certifications that do not constitute material alterations to this appraisal report, such as those required by law or those related to the appraiser's continuing education or membership in an appraisal organization, are permitted.

SCOPE OF WORK: The scope of work for this appraisal is defined by the complexity of this appraisal assignment and the reporting requirements of this appraisal report form, including the following definition of market value, statement of assumptions and limiting conditions, and certifications. The appraiser must, at a minimum: (1) perform a complete visual inspection of the interior and exterior areas of the subject unit, (2) inspect and analyze the condominium project, (3) inspect the neighborhood, (4) inspect each of the comparable sales from at least the street, (5) research, verify, and analyze data from reliable public and/or private sources, and (6) report his or her analysis, opinions, and conclusions in this appraisal report.

INTENDED USE: The intended use of this appraisal report is for the lender/client to evaluate the property that is the subject of this appraisal for a mortgage finance transaction.

INTENDED USER: The intended user of this appraisal report is the lender/client.

MARKET VALUE: The most probable price which a property should bring in a competitive and open market under all conditions requisite to a fair sale, the buyer and seller, each acting prudently, knowledgeably and assuming the price is not affected by undue stimulus. Implicit in this definition is the consummation of a sale as of a specified date and the passing of title from seller to buyer under conditions whereby: (1) buyer and seller are typically motivated; (2) both parties are well informed or well advised, and each acting in what he or she considers his or her own best interest; (3) a reasonable time is allowed for exposure in the open market; (4) payment is made in terms of cash in U. S. dollars or in terms of financial arrangements comparable thereto; and (5) the price represents the normal consideration for the property sold unaffected by special or creative financing or sales concessions* granted by anyone associated with the sale.

*Adjustments to the comparables must be made for special or creative financing or sales concessions. No adjustments are necessary for those costs which are normally paid by sellers as a result of tradition or law in a market area; these costs are readily identifiable since the seller pays these costs in virtually all sales transactions. Special or creative financing adjustments can be made to the comparable property by comparisons to financing terms offered by a third party institutional lender that is not already involved in the property or transaction. Any adjustment should not be calculated on a mechanical dollar for dollar cost of the financing or concession but the dollar amount of any adjustment should approximate the market's reaction to the financing or concessions based on the appraiser's judgment.

STATEMENT OF ASSUMPTIONS AND LIMITING CONDITIONS: The appraiser's certification in this report is subject to the following assumptions and limiting conditions:

1. The appraiser will not be responsible for matters of a legal nature that affect either the property being appraised or the title to it, except for information that he or she became aware of during the research involved in performing this appraisal. The appraiser assumes that the title is good and marketable and will not render any opinions about the title.

2. The appraiser has provided a sketch in this appraisal report to show the approximate dimensions of the improvements. The sketch is included only to assist the reader in visualizing the property and understanding the appraiser's determination of its size.

3. The appraiser has examined the available flood maps that are provided by the Federal Emergency Management Agency (or other data sources) and has noted in this appraisal report whether any portion of the subject site is located in an identified Special Flood Hazard Area. Because the appraiser is not a surveyor, he or she makes no guarantees, express or implied, regarding this determination.

4. The appraiser will not give testimony or appear in court because he or she made an appraisal of the property in question, unless specific arrangements to do so have been made beforehand, or as otherwise required by law.

5. The appraiser has noted in this appraisal report any adverse conditions (such as needed repairs, deterioration, the presence of hazardous wastes, toxic substances, etc.) observed during the inspection of the subject property or that he or she became aware of during the research involved in performing this appraisal. Unless otherwise stated in this appraisal report, the appraiser has no knowledge of any hidden or unapparent physical deficiencies or adverse conditions of the property (such as, but not limited to, needed repairs, deterioration, the presence of hazardous wastes, toxic substances, adverse environmental conditions, etc.) that would make the property less valuable, and has assumed that there are no such conditions and makes no guarantees or warranties, express or implied. The appraiser will not be responsible for any such conditions that do exist or for any engineering or testing that might be required to discover whether such conditions exist. Because the appraiser is not an expert in the field of environmental hazards, this appraisal report must not be considered as an environmental assessment of the property.

6. The appraiser has based his or her appraisal report and valuation conclusion for an appraisal that is subject to satisfactory completion, repairs, or alterations on the assumption that the completion, repairs, or alterations of the subject property will be performed in a professional manner.

Residential appraisal forms

APPRAISER'S CERTIFICATION: The Appraiser certifies and agrees that:

1. I have, at a minimum, developed and reported this appraisal in accordance with the scope of work requirements stated in this appraisal report.

2. I performed a complete visual inspection of the interior and exterior areas of the subject property. I reported the condition of the improvements in factual, specific terms. I identified and reported the physical deficiencies that could affect the livability, soundness, or structural integrity of the property.

3. I performed this appraisal in accordance with the requirements of the Uniform Standards of Professional Appraisal Practice that were adopted and promulgated by the Appraisal Standards Board of The Appraisal Foundation and that were in place at the time this appraisal report was prepared.

4. I developed my opinion of the market value of the real property that is the subject of this report based on the sales comparison approach to value. I have adequate comparable market data to develop a reliable sales comparison approach for this appraisal assignment. I further certify that I considered the cost and income approaches to value but did not develop them, unless otherwise indicated in this report.

5. I researched, verified, analyzed, and reported on any current agreement for sale for the subject property, any offering for sale of the subject property in the twelve months prior to the effective date of this appraisal, and the prior sales of the subject property for a minimum of three years prior to the effective date of this appraisal, unless otherwise indicated in this report.

6. I researched, verified, analyzed, and reported on the prior sales of the comparable sales for a minimum of one year prior to the date of sale of the comparable sale, unless otherwise indicated in this report.

7. I selected and used comparable sales that are locationally, physically, and functionally the most similar to the subject property.

8. I have not used comparable sales that were the result of combining a land sale with the contract purchase price of a home that has been built or will be built on the land.

9. I have reported adjustments to the comparable sales that reflect the market's reaction to the differences between the subject property and the comparable sales.

10. I verified, from a disinterested source, all information in this report that was provided by parties who have a financial interest in the sale or financing of the subject property.

11. I have knowledge and experience in appraising this type of property in this market area.

12. I am aware of, and have access to, the necessary and appropriate public and private data sources, such as multiple listing services, tax assessment records, public land records and other such data sources for the area in which the property is located.

13. I obtained the information, estimates, and opinions furnished by other parties and expressed in this appraisal report from reliable sources that I believe to be true and correct.

14. I have taken into consideration the factors that have an impact on value with respect to the subject neighborhood, subject property, and the proximity of the subject property to adverse influences in the development of my opinion of market value. I have noted in this appraisal report any adverse conditions (such as, but not limited to, needed repairs, deterioration, the presence of hazardous wastes, toxic substances, adverse environmental conditions, etc.) observed during the inspection of the subject property or that I became aware of during the research involved in performing this appraisal. I have considered these adverse conditions in my analysis of the property value, and have reported on the effect of the conditions on the value and marketability of the subject property.

15. I have not knowingly withheld any significant information from this appraisal report and, to the best of my knowledge, all statements and information in this appraisal report are true and correct.

16. I stated in this appraisal report my own personal, unbiased, and professional analysis, opinions, and conclusions, which are subject only to the assumptions and limiting conditions in this appraisal report.

17. I have no present or prospective interest in the property that is the subject of this report, and I have no present or prospective personal interest or bias with respect to the participants in the transaction. I did not base, either partially or completely, my analysis and/or opinion of market value in this appraisal report on the race, color, religion, sex, age, marital status, handicap, familial status, or national origin of either the prospective owners or occupants of the subject property or of the present owners or occupants of the properties in the vicinity of the subject property or on any other basis prohibited by law.

18. My employment and/or compensation for performing this appraisal or any future or anticipated appraisals was not conditioned on any agreement or understanding, written or otherwise, that I would report (or present analysis supporting) a predetermined specific value, a predetermined minimum value, a range or direction in value, a value that favors the cause of any party, or the attainment of a specific result or occurrence of a specific subsequent event (such as approval of a pending mortgage loan application).

19. I personally prepared all conclusions and opinions about the real estate that were set forth in this appraisal report. If I relied on significant real property appraisal assistance from any individual or individuals in the performance of this appraisal or the preparation of this appraisal report, I have named such individual(s) and disclosed the specific tasks performed in this appraisal report. I certify that any individual so named is qualified to perform the tasks. I have not authorized anyone to make a change to any item in this appraisal report; therefore, any change made to this appraisal is unauthorized and I will take no responsibility for it.

20. I identified the lender/client in this appraisal report who is the individual, organization, or agent for the organization that ordered and will receive this appraisal report.

177

Individual Condominium Unit Appraisal Report

21. The lender/client may disclose or distribute this appraisal report to: the borrower; another lender at the request of the borrower; the mortgagee or its successors and assigns; mortgage insurers; government sponsored enterprises; other secondary market participants; data collection or reporting services; professional appraisal organizations; any department, agency, or instrumentality of the United States; and any state, the District of Columbia, or other jurisdictions; without having to obtain the appraiser's or supervisory appraiser's (if applicable) consent. Such consent must be obtained before this appraisal report may be disclosed or distributed to any other party (including, but not limited to, the public through advertising, public relations, news, sales, or other media).

22. I am aware that any disclosure or distribution of this appraisal report by me or the lender/client may be subject to certain laws and regulations. Further, I am also subject to the provisions of the Uniform Standards of Professional Appraisal Practice that pertain to disclosure or distribution by me.

23. The borrower, another lender at the request of the borrower, the mortgagee or its successors and assigns, mortgage insurers, government sponsored enterprises, and other secondary market participants may rely on this appraisal report as part of any mortgage finance transaction that involves any one or more of these parties.

24. If this appraisal report was transmitted as an "electronic record" containing my "electronic signature," as those terms are defined in applicable federal and/or state laws (excluding audio and video recordings), or a facsimile transmission of this appraisal report containing a copy or representation of my signature, the appraisal report shall be as effective, enforceable and valid as if a paper version of this appraisal report were delivered containing my original hand written signature.

25. Any intentional or negligent misrepresentation(s) contained in this appraisal report may result in civil liability and/or criminal penalties including, but not limited to, fine or imprisonment or both under the provisions of Title 18, United States Code, Section 1001, et seq., or similar state laws.

SUPERVISORY APPRAISER'S CERTIFICATION: The Supervisory Appraiser certifies and agrees that:

1. I directly supervised the appraiser for this appraisal assignment, have read the appraisal report, and agree with the appraiser's analysis, opinions, statements, conclusions, and the appraiser's certification.

2. I accept full responsibility for the contents of this appraisal report including, but not limited to, the appraiser's analysis, opinions, statements, conclusions, and the appraiser's certification.

3. The appraiser identified in this appraisal report is either a sub-contractor or an employee of the supervisory appraiser (or the appraisal firm), is qualified to perform this appraisal, and is acceptable to perform this appraisal under the applicable state law.

4. This appraisal report complies with the Uniform Standards of Professional Appraisal Practice that were adopted and promulgated by the Appraisal Standards Board of The Appraisal Foundation and that were in place at the time this appraisal report was prepared.

5. If this appraisal report was transmitted as an "electronic record" containing my "electronic signature," as those terms are defined in applicable federal and/or state laws (excluding audio and video recordings), or a facsimile transmission of this appraisal report containing a copy or representation of my signature, the appraisal report shall be as effective, enforceable and valid as if a paper version of this appraisal report were delivered containing my original hand written signature.

APPRAISER

Signature _____
Name _____
Company Name _____
Company Address _____
_____
Telephone Number _____
Email Address _____
Date of Signature and Report _____
Effective Date of Appraisal _____
State Certification # _____
or State License #_____
or Other _____ State # _____
State _____
Expiration Date of Certification or License _____

ADDRESS OF PROPERTY APPRAISED

_____
_____
APPRAISED VALUE OF SUBJECT PROPERTY $_____
LENDER/CLIENT
Name _____
Company Name _____
Company Address _____
Email Address _____

SUPERVISORY APPRAISER (ONLY IF REQUIRED)

Signature _____
Name _____
Company Name _____
Company Address _____
_____
Telephone Number _____
Email Address _____
Date of Signature _____
State Certification # _____
or State License # _____
State _____
Expiration Date of Certification or License _____

SUBJECT PROPERTY

☐ Did not inspect subject property
☐ Did inspect exterior of subject property from street
   Date of Inspection _____
☐ Did inspect interior and exterior of subject property
   Date of Inspection _____

COMPARABLE SALES

☐ Did not inspect exterior of comparable sales from street
☐ Did inspect exterior of comparable sales from street
   Date of Inspection _____

Residential appraisal forms

Small Residential Income Property Appraisal Report   File

The purpose of this summary appraisal report is to provide the lender/client with an accurate, and adequately supported, opinion of the market value of the subject property.

SUBJECT

Property Address		City	State	Zip Code
Borrower	Owner of Public Record		County	
Legal Description				
Assessor's Parcel #		Tax Year	R.E. Taxes $	
Neighborhood Name		Map Reference	Census Tract	

Occupant ☐ Owner ☐ Tenant ☐ Vacant   Special Assessments $ ☐ PUD HOA $ ☐ per year ☐ per month

Property Rights Appraised ☐ Fee Simple ☐ Leasehold ☐ Other (describe)

Assignment Type ☐ Purchase Transaction ☐ Refinance Transaction ☐ Other (describe)

Lender/Client   Address

Is the subject property currently offered for sale or has it been offered for sale in the twelve months prior to the effective date of this appraisal? ☐ Yes ☐ No

Report data source(s) used, offering price(s), and date(s).

CONTRACT

I ☐ did ☐ did not analyze the contract for sale for the subject purchase transaction. Explain the results of the analysis of the contract for sale or why the analysis was not performed.

Contract Price $ Date of Contract   Is the property seller the owner of public record? ☐ Yes ☐ No Data Source(s)

Is there any financial assistance (loan charges, sale concessions, gift or downpayment assistance, etc.) to be paid by any party on behalf of the borrower? ☐ Yes ☐ No
If Yes, report the total dollar amount and describe the items to be paid.

NEIGHBORHOOD

Note: Race and the racial composition of the neighborhood are not appraisal factors.

Neighborhood Characteristics			2-4 Unit Housing Trends			2-4 Unit Housing		Present Land Use %	
Location ☐ Urban	☐ Suburban	☐ Rural	Property Values ☐ Increasing	☐ Stable	☐ Declining	PRICE	AGE	One-Unit	%
Built-Up ☐ Over 75%	☐ 25–75%	☐ Under 25%	Demand/Supply ☐ Shortage	☐ In Balance	☐ Over Supply	$ (000)	(yrs)	2-4 Unit	%
Growth ☐ Rapid	☐ Stable	☐ Slow	Marketing Time ☐ Under 3 mths	☐ 3–6 mths	☐ Over 6 mths	Low		Multi-Family	%
Neighborhood Boundaries						High		Commercial	%
						Pred.		Other	%

Neighborhood Description

Market Conditions (including support for the above conclusions)

SITE

Dimensions	Area	Shape	View
Specific Zoning Classification	Zoning Description		

Zoning Compliance ☐ Legal ☐ Legal Nonconforming (Grandfathered Use) ☐ No Zoning ☐ Illegal (describe)

Is the highest and best use of the subject property as improved (or as proposed per plans and specifications) the present use? ☐ Yes ☐ No If No, describe

Utilities Public Other (describe)		Public	Other (describe)	Off-site Improvements—Type	Public	Private
Electricity ☐	☐	Water ☐	☐	Street	☐	☐
Gas ☐	☐	Sanitary Sewer ☐	☐	Alley	☐	☐

FEMA Special Flood Hazard Area ☐ Yes ☐ No FEMA Flood Zone   FEMA Map #   FEMA Map Date

Are the utilities and off-site improvements typical for the market area? ☐ Yes ☐ No If No, describe

Are there any adverse site conditions or external factors (easements, encroachments, environmental conditions, land uses, etc.)? ☐ Yes ☐ No If Yes, describe

IMPROVEMENTS

General Description		Foundation		Exterior Description materials/condition	Interior materials/condition	
Units ☐ Two ☐ Three ☐ Four		☐ Concrete Slab ☐ Crawl Space		Foundation Walls	Floors	
☐ Accessory Unit (describe below)		☐ Full Basement ☐ Partial Basement		Exterior Walls	Walls	
# of Stories	# of bldgs.	Basement Area	sq. ft.	Roof Surface	Trim/Finish	
Type ☐ Det. ☐ Att. ☐ S-Det./End Unit		Basement Finish	%	Gutters & Downspouts	Bath Floor	
☐ Existing ☐ Proposed ☐ Under Const.		☐ Outside Entry/Exit ☐ Sump Pump		Window Type	Bath Wainscot	
Design (Style)		Evidence of ☐ Infestation		Storm Sash/Insulated	**Car Storage**	
Year Built		☐ Dampness ☐ Settlement		Screens	☐ None	
Effective Age (Yrs)		**Heating/Cooling**		**Amenities**	☐ Driveway # of Cars	
Attic ☐ None		☐ FWA ☐ HWBB ☐ Radiant		☐ Fireplace(s) # ☐ Woodstove(s) #	Driveway Surface	
☐ Drop Stair ☐ Stairs		☐ Other Fuel		☐ Patio/Deck ☐ Fence	☐ Garage # of Cars	
☐ Floor ☐ Scuttle		☐ Central Air Conditioning		☐ Pool ☐ Porch	☐ Carport # of Cars	
☐ Finished ☐ Heated		☐ Individual ☐ Other		☐ Other	☐ Att. ☐ Det. ☐ Built-in	

# of Appliances ☐ Refrigerator	Range/Oven	☐ Dishwasher	Disposal	Microwave	Washer/Dryer	Other (describe)
Unit # 1 contains:	Rooms	Bedroom(s)	Bath(s)		Square feet of Gross Living Area	
Unit # 2 contains:	Rooms	Bedroom(s)	Bath(s)		Square feet of Gross Living Area	
Unit # 3 contains:	Rooms	Bedroom(s)	Bath(s)		Square feet of Gross Living Area	
Unit # 4 contains:	Rooms	Bedroom(s)	Bath(s)		Square feet of Gross Living Area	

Additional features (special energy efficient items, etc.)

Describe the condition of the property (including needed repairs, deterioration, renovations, remodeling, etc.)

Appendixes

Small Residential Income Property Appraisal Report   File

IMPROVEMENTS

Are there any physical deficiencies or adverse conditions that affect the livability, soundness, or structural integrity of the property? ☐ Yes ☐ No If Yes, describe

Does the property generally conform to the neighborhood (functional utility, style, condition, use, construction, etc.)? ☐ Yes ☐ No If No, describe

Is the property subject to rent control? ☐ Yes ☐ No If Yes, describe

COMPARABLE RENTAL DATA

The following properties represent the most current, similar, and proximate comparable rental properties to the subject property. This analysis is intended to support the opinion of the market rent for the subject property.

FEATURE	SUBJECT	COMPARABLE RENTAL # 1	COMPARABLE RENTAL # 2	COMPARABLE RENTAL # 3
Address				
Proximity to Subject				
Current Monthly Rent	$	$	$	$
Rent/Gross Bldg. Area	$ sq. ft.	$ sq. ft.	$ sq. ft.	$ sq. ft.
Rent Control	☐ Yes ☐ No	☐ Yes ☐ No	☐ Yes ☐ No	☐ Yes ☐ No
Data Source(s)				
Date of Lease(s)				
Location				
Actual Age				
Condition				
Gross Building Area				

Unit Breakdown	Rm Count			Size Sq. Ft.	Rm Count			Size Sq. Ft.	Monthly Rent	Rm Count			Size Sq. Ft.	Monthly Rent	Rm Count			Size Sq. Ft.	Monthly Rent
	Tot	Br	Ba		Tot	Br	Ba			Tot	Br	Ba			Tot	Br	Ba		
Unit # 1									$					$					$
Unit # 2									$					$					$
Unit # 3									$					$					$
Unit # 4									$					$					$
Utilities Included																			

Analysis of rental data and support for estimated market rents for the individual subject units reported below (including the adequacy of the comparables, rental concessions, etc.)

SUBJECT RENT SCHEDULE

Rent Schedule: The appraiser must reconcile the applicable indicated monthly market rents to provide an opinion of the market rent for each unit in the subject property.

	Leases			Actual Rent			Opinion Of Market Rent		
		Lease Date		Per Unit		Total	Per Unit		Total
Unit #	Begin Date	End Date	Unfurnished	Furnished	Rent	Unfurnished	Furnished	Rent
1			$	$	$	$	$	$
2								
3								
4								

Comment on lease data	Total Actual Monthly Rent	$	Total Gross Monthly Rent	$
	Other Monthly Income (itemize)	$	Other Monthly Income (itemize)	$
	Total Actual Monthly Income	$	Total Estimated Monthly Income	$

Utilities included in estimated rents ☐ Electric ☐ Water ☐ Sewer ☐ Gas ☐ Oil ☐ Cable ☐ Trash collection ☐ Other (describe)
Comments on actual or estimated rents and other monthly income (including personal property)

PRIOR SALE HISTORY

I ☐ did ☐ did not research the sale or transfer history of the subject property and comparable sales. If not, explain

My research ☐ did ☐ did not reveal any prior sales or transfers of the subject property for the three years prior to the effective date of this appraisal.
Data source(s)
My research ☐ did ☐ did not reveal any prior sales or transfers of the comparable sales for the year prior to the date of sale of the comparable sale.
Data source(s)
Report the results of the research and analysis of the prior sale history of the subject property and comparable sales (report additional prior sales on page 4).

ITEM	SUBJECT	COMPARABLE SALE # 1	COMPARABLE SALE # 2	COMPARABLE SALE # 3
Date of Prior Sale/Transfer				
Price of Prior Sale/Transfer				
Data Source(s)				
Effective Date of Data Source(s)				

Analysis of prior sale history for the subject property and comparable sales

Residential appraisal forms

Small Residential Income Property Appraisal Report
File #

There are _____ comparable properties currently offered for sale in the subject neighborhood ranging in price from $ _____			to $ _____	
There are _____ comparable sales in the subject neighborhood within the past twelve months ranging in sale price from $ _____			to $ _____	

FEATURE	SUBJECT	COMPARABLE SALE # 1	COMPARABLE SALE # 2	COMPARABLE SALE # 3
Address				
Proximity to Subject				
Sale Price	$	$	$	$
Sale Price/Gross Bldg. Area	$ _____ sq. ft.	$ _____ sq. ft.	$ _____ sq. ft.	$ _____ sq. ft.
Gross Monthly Rent	$	$	$	$
Gross Rent Multiplier				
Price Per Unit	$	$	$	$
Price Per Room	$	$	$	$
Price Per Bedroom	$	$	$	$
Rent Control	☐ Yes ☐ No	☐ Yes ☐ No	☐ Yes ☐ No	☐ Yes ☐ No
Data Source(s)				
Verification Source(s)				

VALUE ADJUSTMENTS	DESCRIPTION	DESCRIPTION	+ (-) Adjustment	DESCRIPTION	+ (-) Adjustment	DESCRIPTION	+ (-) Adjustment
Sale or Financing Concessions							
Date of Sale/Time							
Location							
Leasehold/Fee Simple							
Site							
View							
Design (Style)							
Quality of Construction							
Actual Age							
Condition							
Gross Building Area							
Unit Breakdown	Total Bedrooms Baths	Total Bdrms Baths		Total Bdrms Baths		Total Bdrms Baths	
Unit # 1							
Unit # 2							
Unit # 3							
Unit # 4							
Basement Description							
Basement Finished Rooms							
Functional Utility							
Heating/Cooling							
Energy Efficient Items							
Parking On/Off Site							
Porch/Patio/Deck							
Net Adjustment (Total)		☐ + ☐ -	$	☐ + ☐ -	$	☐ + ☐ -	$
Adjusted Sale Price of Comparables		Net Adj. _____ % Gross Adj. _____ %	$	Net Adj. _____ % Gross Adj. _____ %	$	Net Adj. _____ % Gross Adj. _____ %	$

(S A L E S   C O M P A R I S O N   A P P R O A C H indicated in left margin)

Adj. Price Per Unit (Adj. SP Comp / # of Comp Units)	$			$		$	
Adj. Price Per Room (Adj. SP Comp / # of Comp Rooms)	$			$		$	
Adj. Price Per Bedrm (Adj. SP Comp / # of Comp Bedrooms)	$			$		$	

Value Per Unit	$ _____ X _____ Units = $ _____	Value Per GBA $ _____ X _____ GBA = $ _____
Value Per Rm.	$ _____ X _____ Rooms = $ _____	Value Per Bdrms. $ _____ X _____ Bdrms. = $ _____

Summary of Sales Comparison Approach including reconciliation of the above indicators of value.

Indicated Value by Sales Comparison Approach $ _____

<!-- INCOME section -->
Total gross monthly rent $ _____ X gross rent multiplier (GRM) _____ = $ _____ Indicated value by the Income Approach _____

Comments on income approach including reconciliation of the GRM

Indicated Value by: Sales Comparison Approach $ _____   Income Approach $ _____   Cost Approach (if developed) $ _____

<!-- RECONCILIATION section -->
This appraisal is made ☐ "as is", ☐ subject to completion per plans and specifications on the basis of a hypothetical condition that the improvements have been completed, ☐ subject to the following repairs or alterations on the basis of a hypothetical condition that the repairs or alterations have been completed, or ☐ subject to the following required inspection based on the extraordinary assumption that the condition or deficiency does not require alteration or repair:

Based on a complete visual inspection of the interior and exterior areas of the subject property, defined scope of work, statement of assumptions and limiting conditions, and appraiser's certification, my (our) opinion of the market value, as defined, of the real property that is the subject of this report is $ _____ , as of _____ , which is the date of inspection and the effective date of this appraisal.

Appendixes

Small Residential Income Property Appraisal Report   File

COST APPROACH TO VALUE (not required by Fannie Mae)

Provide adequate information for the lender/client to replicate the below cost figures and calculations.

Support for the opinion of site value (summary of comparable land sales or other methods for estimating site value)

ESTIMATED ☐ REPRODUCTION OR ☐ REPLACEMENT COST NEW	OPINION OF SITE VALUE.. = $
Source of cost data	Dwelling Sq. Ft. @ $ =$
Quality rating from cost service Effective date of cost data	Sq. Ft. @ $ =$
Comments on Cost Approach (gross building area calculations, depreciation, etc.)	
	Garage/Carport Sq. Ft. @ $ =$
	Total Estimate of Cost-New = $
	Less Physical Functional External
	Depreciation =$( )
	Depreciated Cost of Improvements..................................=$
	"As-is" Value of Site Improvements.................................=$
Estimated Remaining Economic Life (HUD and VA only) Years	Indicated Value By Cost Approach..................................=$

PROJECT INFORMATION FOR PUDs (if applicable)

Is the developer/builder in control of the Homeowners' Association (HOA)? ☐ Yes ☐ No   Unit type(s) ☐ Detached ☐ Attached

Provide the following information for PUDs ONLY if the developer/builder is in control of the HOA and the subject property is an attached dwelling unit.

Legal name of project

Total number of phases   Total number of units   Total number of units sold

Total number of units rented   Total number of units for sale   Data source(s)

Was the project created by the conversion of an existing building(s) into a PUD? ☐ Yes ☐ No If Yes, date of conversion

Does the project contain any multi-dwelling units? ☐ Yes ☐ No Data source(s)

Are the units, common elements, and recreation facilities complete? ☐ Yes ☐ No If No, describe the status of completion.

Are the common elements leased to or by the Homeowners' Association? ☐ Yes ☐ No If Yes, describe the rental terms and options.

Describe common elements and recreational facilities.

Residential appraisal forms

Small Residential Income Property Appraisal Report   _{File #}

This report form is designed to report an appraisal of a two- to four-unit property, including a two- to four-unit property in a planned unit development (PUD). A two- to four-unit property located in either a condominium or cooperative project requires the appraiser to inspect the project and complete the project information section of the Individual Condominium Unit Appraisal Report or the Individual Cooperative Interest Appraisal Report and attach it as an addendum to this report.

This appraisal report is subject to the following scope of work, intended use, intended user, definition of market value, statement of assumptions and limiting conditions, and certifications. Modifications, additions, or deletions to the intended use, intended user, definition of market value, or assumptions and limiting conditions are not permitted. The appraiser may expand the scope of work to include any additional research or analysis necessary based on the complexity of this appraisal assignment. Modifications or deletions to the certifications are also not permitted. However, additional certifications that do not constitute material alterations to this appraisal report, such as those required by law or those related to the appraiser's continuing education or membership in an appraisal organization, are permitted.

SCOPE OF WORK: The scope of work for this appraisal is defined by the complexity of this appraisal assignment and the reporting requirements of this appraisal report form, including the following definition of market value, statement of assumptions and limiting conditions, and certifications. The appraiser must, at a minimum: (1) perform a complete visual inspection of the interior and exterior areas of the subject property, (2) inspect the neighborhood, (3) inspect each of the comparable sales from at least the street, (4) research, verify, and analyze data from reliable public and/or private sources, and (5) report his or her analysis, opinions, and conclusions in this appraisal report.

INTENDED USE: The intended use of this appraisal report is for the lender/client to evaluate the property that is the subject of this appraisal for a mortgage finance transaction.

INTENDED USER: The intended user of this appraisal report is the lender/client.

DEFINITION OF MARKET VALUE: The most probable price which a property should bring in a competitive and open market under all conditions requisite to a fair sale, the buyer and seller, each acting prudently, knowledgeably and assuming the price is not affected by undue stimulus. Implicit in this definition is the consummation of a sale as of a specified date and the passing of title from seller to buyer under conditions whereby: (1) buyer and seller are typically motivated; (2) both parties are well informed or well advised, and each acting in what he or she considers his or her own best interest; (3) a reasonable time is allowed for exposure in the open market; (4) payment is made in terms of cash in U. S. dollars or in terms of financial arrangements comparable thereto; and (5) the price represents the normal consideration for the property sold unaffected by special or creative financing or sales concessions* granted by anyone associated with the sale.

*Adjustments to the comparables must be made for special or creative financing or sales concessions. No adjustments are necessary for those costs which are normally paid by sellers as a result of tradition or law in a market area; these costs are readily identifiable since the seller pays these costs in virtually all sales transactions. Special or creative financing adjustments can be made to the comparable property by comparisons to financing terms offered by a third party institutional lender that is not already involved in the property or transaction. Any adjustment should not be calculated on a mechanical dollar for dollar cost of the financing or concession but the dollar amount of any adjustment should approximate the market's reaction to the financing or concessions based on the appraiser's judgment.

STATEMENT OF ASSUMPTIONS AND LIMITING CONDITIONS: The appraiser's certification in this report is subject to the following assumptions and limiting conditions:

1. The appraiser will not be responsible for matters of a legal nature that affect either the property being appraised or the title to it, except for information that he or she became aware of during the research involved in performing this appraisal. The appraiser assumes that the title is good and marketable and will not render any opinions about the title.

2. The appraiser has provided a sketch in this appraisal report to show the approximate dimensions of the improvements, including each of the units. The sketch is included only to assist the reader in visualizing the property and understanding the appraiser's determination of its size.

3. The appraiser has examined the available flood maps that are provided by the Federal Emergency Management Agency (or other data sources) and has noted in this appraisal report whether any portion of the subject site is located in an identified Special Flood Hazard Area. Because the appraiser is not a surveyor, he or she makes no guarantees, express or implied, regarding this determination.

4. The appraiser will not give testimony or appear in court because he or she made an appraisal of the property in question, unless specific arrangements to do so have been made beforehand, or as otherwise required by law.

5. The appraiser has noted in this appraisal report any adverse conditions (such as needed repairs, deterioration, the presence of hazardous wastes, toxic substances, etc.) observed during the inspection of the subject property or that he or she became aware of during the research involved in performing this appraisal. Unless otherwise stated in this appraisal report, the appraiser has no knowledge of any hidden or unapparent physical deficiencies or adverse conditions of the property (such as, but not limited to, needed repairs, deterioration, the presence of hazardous wastes, toxic substances, adverse environmental conditions, etc.) that would make the property less valuable, and has assumed that there are no such conditions and makes no guarantees or warranties, express or implied. The appraiser will not be responsible for any such conditions that do exist or for any engineering or testing that might be required to discover whether such conditions exist. Because the appraiser is not an expert in the field of environmental hazards, this appraisal report must not be considered as an environmental assessment of the property.

6. The appraiser has based his or her appraisal report and valuation conclusion for an appraisal that is subject to satisfactory completion, repairs, or alterations on the assumption that the completion, repairs, or alterations of the subject property will be performed in a professional manner.

Appendixes

Small Residential Income Property Appraisal Report File

APPRAISER'S CERTIFICATION: The Appraiser certifies and agrees that:

1. I have, at a minimum, developed and reported this appraisal in accordance with the scope of work requirements stated in this appraisal report.

2. I performed a complete visual inspection of the interior and exterior areas of the subject property, including all units. I reported the condition of the improvements in factual, specific terms. I identified and reported the physical deficiencies that could affect the livability, soundness, or structural integrity of the property.

3. I performed this appraisal in accordance with the requirements of the Uniform Standards of Professional Appraisal Practice that were adopted and promulgated by the Appraisal Standards Board of The Appraisal Foundation and that were in place at the time this appraisal report was prepared.

4. I developed my opinion of the market value of the real property that is the subject of this report based on the sales comparison and income approaches to value. I have adequate market data to develop reliable sales comparison and income approaches to value for this appraisal assignment. I further certify that I considered the cost approach to value but did not develop it, unless otherwise indicated in this report.

5. I researched, verified, analyzed, and reported on any current agreement for sale for the subject property, any offering for sale of the subject property in the twelve months prior to the effective date of this appraisal, and the prior sales of the subject property for a minimum of three years prior to the effective date of this appraisal, unless otherwise indicated in this report.

6. I researched, verified, analyzed, and reported on the prior sales of the comparable sales for a minimum of one year prior to the date of sale of the comparable sale, unless otherwise indicated in this report.

7. I selected and used comparable sales that are locationally, physically, and functionally the most similar to the subject property.

8. I have not used comparable sales that were the result of combining a land sale with the contract purchase price of a home that has been built or will be built on the land.

9. I have reported adjustments to the comparable sales that reflect the market's reaction to the differences between the subject property and the comparable sales.

10. I verified, from a disinterested source, all information in this report that was provided by parties who have a financial interest in the sale or financing of the subject property.

11. I have knowledge and experience in appraising this type of property in this market area.

12. I am aware of, and have access to, the necessary and appropriate public and private data sources, such as multiple listing services, tax assessment records, public land records and other such data sources for the area in which the property is located.

13. I obtained the information, estimates, and opinions furnished by other parties and expressed in this appraisal report from reliable sources that I believe to be true and correct.

14. I have taken into consideration the factors that have an impact on value with respect to the subject neighborhood, subject property, and the proximity of the subject property to adverse influences in the development of my opinion of market value. I have noted in this appraisal report any adverse conditions (such as, but not limited to, needed repairs, deterioration, the presence of hazardous wastes, toxic substances, adverse environmental conditions, etc.) observed during the inspection of the subject property or that I became aware of during the research involved in performing this appraisal. I have considered these adverse conditions in my analysis of the property value, and have reported on the effect of the conditions on the value and marketability of the subject property.

15. I have not knowingly withheld any significant information from this appraisal report and, to the best of my knowledge, all statements and information in this appraisal report are true and correct.

16. I stated in this appraisal report my own personal, unbiased, and professional analysis, opinions, and conclusions, which are subject only to the assumptions and limiting conditions in this appraisal report.

17. I have no present or prospective interest in the property that is the subject of this report, and I have no present or prospective personal interest or bias with respect to the participants in the transaction. I did not base, either partially or completely, my analysis and/or opinion of market value in this appraisal report on the race, color, religion, sex, age, marital status, handicap, familial status, or national origin of either the prospective owners or occupants of the subject property or of the present owners or occupants of the properties in the vicinity of the subject property or on any other basis prohibited by law.

18. My employment and/or compensation for performing this appraisal or any future or anticipated appraisals was not conditioned on any agreement or understanding, written or otherwise, that I would report (or present analysis supporting) a predetermined specific value, a predetermined minimum value, a range or direction in value, a value that favors the cause of any party, or the attainment of a specific result or occurrence of a specific subsequent event (such as approval of a pending mortgage loan application).

19. I personally prepared all conclusions and opinions about the real estate that were set forth in this appraisal report. If I relied on significant real property appraisal assistance from any individual or individuals in the performance of this appraisal or the preparation of this appraisal report, I have named such individual(s) and disclosed the specific tasks performed in this appraisal report. I certify that any individual so named is qualified to perform the tasks. I have not authorized anyone to make a change to any item in this appraisal report; therefore, any change made to this appraisal is unauthorized and I will take no responsibility for it.

20. I identified the lender/client in this appraisal report who is the individual, organization, or agent for the organization that ordered and will receive this appraisal report.

Residential appraisal forms

Small Residential Income Property Appraisal Report   File

21. The lender/client may disclose or distribute this appraisal report to: the borrower; another lender at the request of the borrower; the mortgagee or its successors and assigns; mortgage insurers; government sponsored enterprises; other secondary market participants; data collection or reporting services; professional appraisal organizations; any department, agency, or instrumentality of the United States; and any state, the District of Columbia, or other jurisdictions; without having to obtain the appraiser's or supervisory appraiser's (if applicable) consent. Such consent must be obtained before this appraisal report may be disclosed or distributed to any other party (including, but not limited to, the public through advertising, public relations, news, sales, or other media).

22. I am aware that any disclosure or distribution of this appraisal report by me or the lender/client may be subject to certain laws and regulations. Further, I am also subject to the provisions of the Uniform Standards of Professional Appraisal Practice that pertain to disclosure or distribution by me.

23. The borrower, another lender at the request of the borrower, the mortgagee or its successors and assigns, mortgage insurers, government sponsored enterprises, and other secondary market participants may rely on this appraisal report as part of any mortgage finance transaction that involves any one or more of these parties.

24. If this appraisal report was transmitted as an "electronic record" containing my "electronic signature," as those terms are defined in applicable federal and/or state laws (excluding audio and video recordings), or a facsimile transmission of this appraisal report containing a copy or representation of my signature, the appraisal report shall be as effective, enforceable and valid as if a paper version of this appraisal report were delivered containing my original hand written signature.

25. Any intentional or negligent misrepresentation(s) contained in this appraisal report may result in civil liability and/or criminal penalties including, but not limited to, fine or imprisonment or both under the provisions of Title 18, United States Code, Section 1001, et seq., or similar state laws.

SUPERVISORY APPRAISER'S CERTIFICATION: The Supervisory Appraiser certifies and agrees that:

1. I directly supervised the appraiser for this appraisal assignment, have read the appraisal report, and agree with the appraiser's analysis, opinions, statements, conclusions, and the appraiser's certification.

2. I accept full responsibility for the contents of this appraisal report including, but not limited to, the appraiser's analysis, opinions, statements, conclusions, and the appraiser's certification.

3. The appraiser identified in this appraisal report is either a sub-contractor or an employee of the supervisory appraiser (or the appraisal firm), is qualified to perform this appraisal, and is acceptable to perform this appraisal under the applicable state law.

4. This appraisal report complies with the Uniform Standards of Professional Appraisal Practice that were adopted and promulgated by the Appraisal Standards Board of The Appraisal Foundation and that were in place at the time this appraisal report was prepared.

5. If this appraisal report was transmitted as an "electronic record" containing my "electronic signature," as those terms are defined in applicable federal and/or state laws (excluding audio and video recordings), or a facsimile transmission of this appraisal report containing a copy or representation of my signature, the appraisal report shall be as effective, enforceable and valid as if a paper version of this appraisal report were delivered containing my original hand written signature.

APPRAISER

Signature _____
Name _____
Company Name_____
Company Address _____
_____
Telephone Number _____
Email Address _____
Date of Signature and Report _____
Effective Date of Appraisal_____
State Certification # _____
or State License # _____
or Other (describe)_____ State # _____
State_____
Expiration Date of Certification or License _____

ADDRESS OF PROPERTY APPRAISED

_____
_____

APPRAISED VALUE OF SUBJECT PROPERTY $ _____

LENDER/CLIENT

Name _____
Company Name_____
Company Address _____
_____
Email Address _____

SUPERVISORY APPRAISER (ONLY IF REQUIRED)

Signature _____
Name _____
Company Name _____
Company Address _____
_____
Telephone Number_____
Email Address _____
Date of Signature _____
State Certification # _____
or State License # _____
State_____
Expiration Date of Certification or License_____

SUBJECT PROPERTY

☐ Did not inspect subject property
☐ Did inspect exterior of subject property from street
    Date of Inspection _____
☐ Did inspect interior and exterior of subject property
    Date of Inspection_____

COMPARABLE SALES

☐ Did not inspect exterior of comparable sales from street
☐ Did inspect exterior of comparable sales from street
    Date of Inspection_____

Appendix 7
Where to reach for help in the United States and Canada

When you first start in this industry, you often begin with a blank slate without a network of professionals on whom to call. However, if you have listened to the advice of the experts interviewed for this book, you are working hard with your mentor at developing a strong reputation for yourself.

Your mentor will probably help you develop a strong network by introducing you to his or her network and industry experts. That will get your network off and running.

You are also likely to be a member of, and quickly getting involved in, a local chapter of a real estate appraising organization such as the Appraisal Institute (AI) or the National Association of Real Estate Appraisers (NAREA). These two organizations have dozens of chapters across the country, providing you with the opportunity to network and learn from the best in the industry.

About 71,000 licensed real estate appraisers work in the United States. The organization with the largest number of members is the

Appraisal Institute, which has a membership of about 18,000 and includes about 100 local chapters across the United States, Canada, and abroad.

The AI provides education, research, publishing, and professional membership for both residential and commercial appraisers. It also houses the Lim Library, a storehouse of appraisal research information for AI members and the industry as a whole. The AI also awards two of the most sought-after professional designations in the industry, the MAI and SRA.

For more information about the AI, visit the organization's Web site at www.appraisalinstitute.org.

The National Association of Real Estate Appraisers (NAREA) is one of the largest real estate appraiser organizations in the country. NAREA develops and presents education programs for its members, and it holds an annual Appraisal Expo and Conference. It also publishes information such as updates to appraiser regulations for its members.

For more information about NAREA, visit its Web site at www.iami.org/narea.cfm.

Appraisers are also members of other appraisal organizations, including

- The National Association of Realtors Appraisal Section (www.realtor.org)
- International Right of Way Association (www.irwaonline.org)
- American Society of Appraisers (www.appraisers.org)
- American Society of Farm Managers and Rural Appraisers (www.asfmra.org)
- International Association of Assessing Officers (www.iaao.org)
- National Association of Independent Fee Appraisers (www.naifa.com)

Another Web site frequented by appraisers who wish to learn about the newest Uniform Standards of Professional Appraisal Practice (USPAP) regulations is www.appraisalfoundation.org.

Residential appraisers also frequent www.fanniemae.com to locate the most up-to-date appraisal forms.

In Canada

Resources for appraisers in Canada include the following.

Canadian National Association of Real Estate Appraisers (www.cnarea.ca/)—a national, not-for-profit, independent association that certifies and regulates real property appraisers.

Nova Scotia Real Estate Appraisers Association (www.nsappraisal.ns.ca/)—anyone engaged in the practice of real estate appraisal within the meaning of the Act must be a registered member of the Nova Scotia Real Estate Appraisers Association.

Ontario Association of the Appraisal Institute of Canada (www.oaaic.on.ca/)—The Ontario Association of the Appraisal Institute of Canada, is the largest organization of real estate appraisers, valuators, and property consultants in Ontario.

Appendix 8
Local appraiser regulations

Use the following Web sites and phone numbers to find out the specific regulations in your state.

Alabama Real Estate Appraisers Board
www.reab.state.al.us/   334-242-8747

Alaska Board of Certified Real Estate Appraisers
www.dced.state.ak.us/occ/papr.htm   907-465-2542

Arizona Board of Appraisal
www.appraisal.state.az.us/   602-542-1539

Arkansas Appraiser Licensing & Certification Board
www.state.ar.us/alcb/   501-296-1843

California Office of Real Estate Appraisers
www.orea.ca.gov/   916-552-9000

Colorado Board of Real Estate Appraisers
www.dora.state.co.us/real-estate/appraisr/appraisr.htm
303-894-2166

Connecticut Real Estate Appraisal Commission
www.ct.gov/dcp/cwp/view.asp?a=1622&Q=287752&PM=1
860-713-6150

DC Board of Appraisers
www.dcra.dc.gov/dcra/site/default.asp   202-442-4320

Delaware Real Estate Appraiser Certification
www.professionallicensing.state.de.us/boards/realestateappraisers
/index.shtml   302-739 4522

Florida Real Estate Appraisal Board
www.state.fl.us/dbpr/re/freab_welcome.shtml   407-245-0800

Georgia Real Estate Appraiser Board
www.grec.state.ga.us/   404-656-3916

Hawaii Appraisal Advisory Committee
www.hawaii.gov/dcca/areas/pvl/programs/realestateappraiser/
808-586-2704

Idaho Certified Real Estate Appraiser Board
www.ibol.idaho.gov/   208-334-3233

Illinois Office of Banks and Real Estate
www.idfpr.com/dpr/re/APPRAISAL.asp   217-785-9634

Indiana Real Estate Appraiser Certification Board
www.in.gov/pla/bandc/appraiser/   317-232-2980

Iowa Real Estate Appraiser Board
www.state.ia.us/government/com/prof/appraiser/home.html
515-281-7363

Kansas Real Estate Appraisal Board
www.accesskansas.org/kreab/   785-271-3373

Kentucky Real Estate Appraisers Board
www.kreab.ky.gov/   859-543-8943

Louisiana Real Estate Appraisal Subcommittee
www.lreasbc.state.la.us   225-765-0191

Maine Board of Real Estate Appraisers
www.state.me.us/pfr/olr/categories/cat37.htm   207-624-8520

Maryland State Commission of Real Estate Appraisers
www.dllr.state.md.us/license/occprof/reappr.html   410-230-6165

Massachusetts Board of Registration of Real Estate Appraisers
www.mass.gov/dpl/boards/ra/index.htm   617-727-3055

Michigan Real Estate Appraisers Board
www.michigan.gov/cis/0,1607,7-154-10557_12992_13893——,00.html
517-241-9201

Minnesota Real Estate Appraisers Advisory Board
www.state.mn.us/portal/mn/jsp/home.do?agency=Commerce
651-296-6319

Mississippi Appraisal Board
www.mrec.state.ms.us/   601-932-9191

Missouri State Real Estate Appraisers Commission
www.pr.mo.gov/appraisers.asp   573-751-0038

Montana Board of Real Estate Appraisers
www.discoveringmontana.com/dli/bsd/license/bsd_boards/rea_board/
licenses/rea/lic_summary.asp   406-841-2381

Nebraska Real Estate Appraiser Board
www.appraiser.ne.gov/   402-471-9015

Nevada Real Estate Appraisal Commission
www.red.state.nv.us/   775-687-4280

New Hampshire Real Estate Appraiser Board
www.state.nh.us/nhreab/   603-271-6186

New Jersey Board of Real Estate Appraisers
www.state.nj.us/lps/ca/nonmedical/reappraisers.htm
973-504-6480

New Mexico Real Estate Appraisers Board
www.rld.state.nm.us/b&c/reappraisers/index.htm   505-476-7053

New York State Board of Real Estate Appraisal
www.dos.state.ny.us/lcns/appraise.htm   518-473-2728

North Carolina Real Estate Appraisal Board
www.ncappraisalboard.org/   919-420-7920

North Dakota Real Estate Appraisal Qualification And Ethics Board
www.governor.state.nd.us/boards/boards-query.asp?Board_ID=92
701-222-1051

Ohio Real Estate Appraiser Board
www.com.state.oh.us/real/appmain.htm   614-466-3475

Oklahoma Appraiser Board
www.oid.state.ok.us/agentbrokers/realestate.html   405-521-6636

Oregon Appraiser Certification & Licensure Board
www.oregonaclb.org/   503-485-2555

Pennsylvania State Board of Certified Real Estate Appraisers
www.dos.state.pa.us/bpoa/cwp/browse.asp?A=1104   717-783-4866

Puerto Rico Board of Real Estate Appraisers
www.estado.gobierno.pr/evaluado.htm   787-723-2121

Rhode Island Real Estate Appraisers Board
www.dbr.state.ri.us/real_estate.html   401-222-2262

South Carolina Appraiser Board
www.llr.state.sc.us/POL/RealEstateAppraisers/   803-896-4400

South Dakota Appraiser Advisory Board
www.state.sd.us/drr2/reg/appraisers/   605-773-4608

Tennessee Real Estate Appraiser Commission
www.state.tn.us/commerce/boards/treac/index.html   615-741-1831

Texas Appraiser Licensing and Certification Board
www.talcb.state.tx.us/AgencyInfo/default.asp   512-465-3950

Utah Real Estate Appraiser & Registration Certification Board
www.commerce.utah.gov/dre/applicensing.html   801-530-6747

Vermont Real Estate Appraisal Board
www.vtprofessionals.org/opr1/appraisers/   802-828-3228

Virginia Real Estate Appraiser Board
www.state.va.us/dpor/apr_main.htm   804-367-8552

Washington Real Estate Appraiser Advisory Committee
www.dol.wa.gov/app/appfront.htm   360-664-6504

Local appraiser regulations

West Virginia Real Estate Appraiser Advisory Committee
www.wvs.state.wv.us/appraise/   304-558-3919

Wisconsin Appraiser Board
drl.wi.gov/index.htm   608-266-5511

Wyoming Real Estate Appraiser Certification Board
realestate.state.wy.us/   307-777-7141

Appendix 9
Glossary of real estate appraisal terms

This Glossary is reprinted with permission of the Appraisal Connection, Inc., residential real estate appraisals and consultants, Miami, Florida.

A

Abstract   A history of all transactions shown in the public records affecting a particular tract of land.

Abstract Plant   Also called "Title Plant" in some areas. A geographically filed assemblage of title information that helps in expediting title examinations, such as copies of previous attorneys' opinions, abstracts, tax searches, and copies of take-offs of the public records.

Acceleration Clause   Condition in a mortgage that may require the balance of the loan to become due immediately if regular mortgage payments are not made or for breach of other conditions of the mortgage.

Adjustable Rate Mortgage (ARM)   Mortgage loans under which the interest rate is periodically adjusted, in accordance with some market indicator, to more closely coincide with the current rates. The extent and number of these adjustments are agreed to at the inception of the loan.

Adverse Possession   The possession, by one person, of land belonging to another in a manner deemed adverse to the interest of the owner. In most states, by operation of law, title to the land becomes vested in such person after a fixed number of years if the owner fails to assert his or her rights.

Affidavit   A written statement made under oath before a notary public or other judicial officer.

Agreement   A legally binding contract made between two or more persons.

ALTA (American Land Title Association)   The trade association of the title insurance industry, which has adopted certain insurance policy forms to standardize coverage on a national basis.

Amortization   Payment to reduce the principal of a debt in regular, periodic installments.

Appraisal   A report from an independent third party detailing the estimated value of real estate.

Appurtenance   A right or privilege that is a part of the ownership of property, such as a right of way to a highway across the land of another. Water rights are also an example.

Assessment   (1) The valuation of real estate for purposes of taxes or special improvement charges. (2) The amount of taxes or special improvement charges. Special improvement charges are usually for the costs of streets, sidewalks, sewers, etc.

Assignment   (1) The act of transferring an interest, such as a loan secured by a mortgage, from one person to another. (2) The instrument or paper by which one person transfers such ownership to another.

Assumption of Mortgage   An obligation undertaken by the purchaser of property to be personally liable for payment of an existing mortgage. In an assumption, the purchaser is substituted for the original mortgagor in the mortgage instrument and the original mortgagor is to be released from further liability in the assumption, the mortgagee's consent is usually required.

The original mortgagor should always obtain a written release from further liability if he desires to be fully released under the assumption. Failure to obtain such a release renders the original mortgagor liable if the person assuming the mortgage fails to make the monthly payments.

An "Assumption of Mortgage" is often confused with "Purchasing Subject to a Mortgage." When one purchases subject to a mortgage, the purchaser agrees to make the monthly mortgage payments on an existing mortgage, but the original mortgagor remains personally liable if the purchaser fails to make the monthly payments. Since the original mortgagor remains liable in the event of default, the mortgagee's consent is not required to a sale subject to a mortgage.

Both "Assumption of Mortgage" and "Purchasing Subject to a Mortgage" are used to finance the sale of property. They may also be used when a mortgagor is in financial difficulty and desires to sell the property to avoid foreclosure.

Attorney's Opinion   A statement by an attorney as to the validity of a title, arrived at after investigation of the history of the title as recorded in the public records.

B

Back Title Letter   Also called "Back Title Certificate" in some areas, and "Starter" in others. When titles previously have been examined up to a certain date by reliable examiners, title companies sometimes give subsequent examiners of such titles a letter that sets forth the condition of the title at the time of the previous examination and authorizes them to begin their subsequent examination with the terminal date of the previous examination.

Balloon Note   A form of promissory note that calls for the minimum payment of principal and the payment of interest at regular intervals. This type of note requires a substantial final payment, which represents all the principal.

Bankruptcy   A proceeding in the U.S. District Court wherein assets of an insolvent debtor are protected and distributed in an equitable manner.

Binder Sometimes called a "Preliminary Certificate" or "Commitment." (1) A preliminary report as to the condition of a title and a commitment to issue a title insurance policy in a certain manner when certain conditions are met. (2) A deposit in escrow of a small part of the purchase price of real estate as evidence of good faith and to bind an agreement to purchase.

Broker Also known as a "Real Estate Broker." A middleman or agent who buys and sells real estate for a company, firm, or individual on a commission basis. The broker does not have title to the property, but generally represents the owner.

Building Line or Setback Distances from the ends and/or sides of the lot beyond which construction may not extend. The building line may be established by a filed plat of subdivision, by restrictive covenants in deeds or leases, by building codes, or by zoning ordinances.

C

Certificate of Title A certificate issued by a title examiner stating the condition of a title.

Chain In real estate measurements (surveying), a chain is 66 feet long or 100 links, each link being 7.92 inches. The measurement may change when used in fields other than surveying.

Chain of Title The successive ownerships or transfers in the history of title to a tract of land.

Claim An adverse right or interest asserted by one part against another or against an insurer or inseminator. Claims may arise from unpaid debts or taxes, as well as from hidden title defects such as fraud, forgery, missing heirs, etc.

Clear Title Real property ownership free of liens, defects, encumbrances, or claims.

Closing Also called "Settlement." A meeting of all parties involved in a property transaction during which the transaction is consummated.

Closing Costs The numerous expenses which buyers and sellers normally incur to complete a transaction in the transfer of ownership of real estate. These costs are in addition to price of the property and are items prepaid at the closing day. This is a typical list:

BUYER'S EXPENSES	SELLER'S EXPENSES
• Documentary Stamps on Notes	• Cost of Abstract
• Recording Deed and Mortgage	• Documentary Stamps on Deed
• Escrow Fees	• Real Estate Commission
• Attorney's Fee	• Recording Mortgage
• Title Insurance	• Survey Charge
• Appraisal and Inspection	• Escrow Fees
• Survey Charge	• Attorney's Fee

The agreement of sale negotiated previously between the buyer and the seller may state in writing who will pay each of the above costs.

Closing Day   The day on which the formalities of a real estate sale are concluded. The certificate of title, abstract, and deed are generally prepared for the closing by an attorney and this cost charged to the buyer. The buyer signs the mortgage, and closing costs are paid. The final closing merely confirms the original agreement reached in the agreement of sale.

Clouded Title   An irregularity, possible claim, or encumbrance that, if valid, would adversely affect or impair the title.

Coinsurance   Two or more policies of title insurance issued by different insurers, each covering a portion of the same risk, which together provide total coverage of the risk.

Commission   Money paid to a real estate agent or broker by the seller as compensation for finding a buyer and completing the sale. Usually it is a percentage of the sale price—6 to 7 percent on houses, 10 percent on land.

Commitment   Also called a "Binder." A document issued by a title insurance company that contains the conditions under which a policy of title insurance will be issued.

Condemnation   (1) The taking of private property for a public purpose, with compensation to the owner under the right of eminent domain. Governmental units, railroads, and utility companies have the right to condemn and take private property. (2) The destruction by government of private property that imperils the life, health, or safety of the public.

Condominium Individual ownership of a dwelling unit and an individual interest in the common areas and facilities that serve the multi-unit project.

Commitment Also called a "Binder." A document issued by a title insurance company that contains the conditions under which a policy of title insurance will be issued.

Conventional Mortgage A mortgage loan not insured by HUD or guaranteed by the Veterans' Administration. It is subject to conditions established by the lending institution and state statutes. The mortgage rates may vary with different institutions and between states. (States have various interest limits.)

Conveyance The transfer of title to property from one person to another.

Cooperative Housing An apartment building or a group of dwellings owned by a corporation, the stockholders of which are the residents of the dwellings. It is operated for their benefit by their elected board of directors. In a cooperative, the corporation or association owns title to the real estate. A resident purchases stock in the corporation, which entitles him to occupy a unit in the building or property owned by the cooperative. While the resident does not own his unit, he has an absolute right to occupy his unit for as long as he owns the stock.

Covenant A formal agreement or contract between two parties in which one party gives the other certain promises and assurances, such as covenants of warranty in a warranty deed.

Curtesy A right that a husband has in his wife's property at her death. It does not exist in all states.

D

Dedication The setting aside of certain land by the owner and declaring it to be for public use. Examples: streets, sidewalks, parks, etc.

Deed   A formal written instrument by which title to real property is transferred from one owner to another. The deed should contain an accurate description of the property being conveyed, should be signed and witnessed according to the laws of the state where the property is located, and should be delivered to the purchaser at closing day. There are two parties to a deed: the grantor and the grantee. (See also Deed of Trust, General Warranty Deed, Quitclaim Deed, and Special Warranty Deed.)

Deed of Trust   Like a mortgage, a security instrument whereby real property is given as security for a debt. However, in a deed of trust there are three parties to the instrument: the borrower, the trustee, and the lender (or beneficiary). In such a transaction, the borrower transfers the legal title for the property to the trustee who holds the property in trust as security for the payment of the debt to the lender or beneficiary. If the borrower pays the debt as agreed, the deed of trust becomes void. If, however, he or she defaults in the payment of the debt, the trustee may sell the property at a public sale, under the terms of the deed of trust. In most jurisdictions where the deed of trust is in force, the borrower is subject to having his or her property sold without benefit of legal proceedings. A few states have begun in recent years to treat the deed of trust like a mortgage.

Deed Restriction   A covenant contained in a deed imposing limits on the use or occupancy of the real estate or the type, size, purpose, or location of improvements to be constructed on it.

Default   Failure to make mortgage payments as agreed to in a commitment based on the terms and at the designated time set forth in the mortgage or deed of trust. It is the mortgagor's responsibility to remember the due date and send the payment prior to the due date, not after. Generally, 30 days after the due date if payment is not received, the mortgage is in default. In the event of default, the mortgage may give the lender the right to accelerate payments, take possession and receive rents, and start foreclosure. Defaults may also come about by the failure to observe other conditions in the mortgage or deed of trust.

Defect   A blemish, imperfection, or deficiency. A defective title is one that is irregular and faulty.

Depreciation   Loss in value occasioned by ordinary wear and tear, destructive action of the elements, or functional or economic obsolescence.

Devise   A gift of real estate made by a will.

Documentary Stamps   A state tax, in the forms of stamps, required on deeds and mortgages when real estate title passes from one owner to another. The amount of stamps required varies with each state.

Dominant Estate   The property for the benefit of which a right-of-way easement exists across another's adjoining piece of land is said to be the dominant estate. The land across which the easement runs is said to be the servant estate.

Dower   A right that a wife has in her husband's property at the time of his death. Does not exist in all states.

Down Payment   The amount of money to be paid by the purchaser to the seller upon the signing of the agreement of sale. The agreement of sale will refer to the down payment amount and will acknowledge receipt of the down payment. Down payment is the difference between the sales price and maximum mortgage amount. The down payment may not be refundable if the purchaser fails to buy the property without good cause. If the purchaser wants the down payment to be refundable, he or she should insert a clause in the agreement of sale specifying the conditions under which the deposit will be refunded, if the agreement does not already contain such clause. If the seller cannot deliver good title, the agreement of sale usually requires the seller to return the down payment and to pay interest and expenses incurred by the purchaser.

E

Earnest Money   The deposit money given to the seller or his agent by the potential buyer upon the signing of the agreement of sale to show that he or she is serious about buying the house. If the sale goes through, the earnest money is applied against the down payment. If the sale does not go through, the earnest money will be forfeited or lost unless the binder or offer to purchase expressly provides that it is refundable.

Easement   A right to use all or part of the land owned by another for a specific purpose. An easement may, for example, entitle its holder to install and maintain sewer or utility lines.

Eminent Domain   The right of a government to take privately owned property for public purposes under condemnation proceedings subject to payment of its fair market value.

Encroachment   Any building, improvement, or structure located on one property (such as a wall, fence, or driveway) that intrudes upon the property of another.

Encumbrance   Any interest, right, lien, or liability attached to a parcel of land (such as unpaid taxes or an unsatisfied mortgage) that constitutes or represents a burden or charge upon the property.

Equity   The value of a homeowner's unencumbered interest in real estate. Equity is computed by subtracting from the property's fair market value the total of the unpaid mortgage balance and any outstanding liens or other debts against the property. A homeowner's equity increases as he or she pays off his or her mortgage or as the property appreciates in value. When the mortgage and all other debts against the property are paid in full the homeowner has 100 percent equity in his or her property.

Escheat   The reversion of property to the state when an owner dies leaving no legal heirs, devises, or claimants.

Escrow   Funds paid by one party to another (the escrow agent) to hold until the occurrence of a specified event, after which the funds are released to a designated individual. In FHA mortgage transactions an escrow account usually refers to the funds a mortgagor pays the lender at the time of the periodic mortgage payments. The money is held in a trust fund provided by the lender for the buyer. Such funds should be adequate to cover yearly anticipated expenditures for mortgage insurance premiums, taxes, hazard insurance premiums, and special assessments.

Estoppel   A legal restraint that stops or prevents a person from contradicting or reneging on his or her previous position or previous assertions or commitments.

Examination   The study of the instruments and muniments incident to a chain of title to determine their effect and condition in order to reach a conclusion as to the status of title.

Exception   A provision in a title insurance binder or policy that excludes liability for a specific title defect or an outstanding lien or encumbrance.

Execute   To sign a legal instrument. A deed is said to be executed when it is signed, sealed, witnessed, and delivered

F

Fannie Mae (FNMA)   Federal National Mortgage Association. A private corporation dealing in the purchase of first mortgages.

Fee Simple Deed   The absolute ownership of a parcel of land. The highest degree of ownership that a person can have in real estate, which gives the owner unqualified ownership and full power.

FHA (Federal Housing Administration)   A federal agency that insures first mortgages, enabling lenders to lend a very high percentage of the sale price.

Fixed Rate Mortgage   A mortgage having a rate of interest that remains the same for the life of the mortgage.

Fixtures   Personal property that is attached to real property and is legally treated as real property while it is so attached. Examples: medicine cabinets, window blinds, and chandeliers.

Foreclosure   A legal term applied to any of the various methods of enforcing payment of the debt secured by a mortgage, or deed of trust, by taking and selling the mortgaged property and depriving the mortgagor of possession.

Forgery   The fraudulent signing of another's name to an instrument such as a deed, mortgage, or check.

Freddie Mac (FHLMC)   Federal Home Loan Mortgage Corporation. A federal agency that purchases both conventional and federally insured first mortgages from members of the Federal Reserve System and the Federal Loan Bank System.

G

General Warranty Deed   A deed that conveys not only all the grantor's interests in and title to the property to the grantee, but also warrants that if the title is defective or has a "cloud" on it (such as mortgage claims, tax liens, title claims, judgments, or mechanic's liens against it) the grantee may hold the grantor liable.

Ginnie Mae (GNMA)   Government National Mortgage Association. A federal association working with the FHA that offers special assistance in obtaining mortgages and purchases mortgages in the secondary market.

Grant   To bestow or confer, with or without compensation, a gift such as land or money by one having control or authority over the gift.

Grantee   One to whom a grant is made.

Grantor   One who makes a grant.

H

Hereditaments   Any and all kinds of estates, interest, and rights in real estate that can be inherited.

Homeowners Insurance   Real estate insurance protecting against loss caused by fire, some natural causes, vandalism, etc., depending on the terms of the policy. Also includes coverage such as personal liability and theft away from home.

HUD (Department of Housing and Urban Development)   The federal department responsible for the major housing programs in the United States.

I

Index   (1) An alphabetical listing in the public records of the names of parties to a recorded real estate instrument together with the book and page number of the record. (2) The listing in abstract and title plants of recorded real estate instruments in groups according to land descriptions, known as geographical index. (3) The alphabetical listing in abstract and title plants, by names of the parties, of all recorded instruments that affect but do not describe particular real estate, such as judgments, powers of attorney, wills, and probate proceedings. Such indexes are known by various names, such as "General Index," "Judgment Index," and "Name Index."

Instrument   Any written document having a legal effect.

Interest   A charge paid for borrowing money. (See also Mortgage Note.)

J

Judgment   The determination of a court regarding the rights of parties in an action. A judgment of debt on a property owner can create a lien on all of that owner's land within a certain jurisdiction.

Junior Mortgage   A mortgage lower in lien priority than another.

K

L

Leasehold   The right to possession and use of land for a fixed period of time. The lease is the agreement that creates the right.

Lessee   A tenant holding a leasehold.

Lessor   A landlord; one who gives a leasehold to a lessee.

License   Permission to go upon or use the land of another, the permission being a personal privilege and not constituting an interest in the land.

Lien   A claim by one person on the property of another as security for money owed. Such claims may include obligations not met or satisfied, judgments, unpaid taxes, materials, or labor. (See also Special Lien.)

Lien Waiver   Also called a "Waiver of Liens." A waiver of mechanics' lien rights, signed by contractors or subcontractors.

Link   In surveying, a link is 7.92 inches.

Loan Policy   Also called a "Mortgagee Policy." A title insurance policy insuring a mortgagee, or beneficiary under a deed of trust, against loss caused by invalidity or unenforceability of a lien, or loss of priority of the mortgage or deed of trust.

Lis Pendens   A legal notice intending to bind third parties of litigation claiming an interest in real estate.

Lot   Generally, a portion of a parcel of real property. Usually refers to a portion of a subdivision.

M

Market Value   The average of the highest price that a buyer, willing but not compelled to buy, would pay, and the lowest price a seller, willing but not compelled to sell, would accept.

Marketable Title   A title that is free and clear of objectionable liens, clouds, or other title defects. A title that enables an owner to sell his or her property freely to others and that others will accept without objection.

Mechanic's Lien   A lien on real estate, created by operation of law, that secures the payment of debts due to persons who perform labor or services or furnish materials incident to the construction of buildings and improvements on the real estate.

Metes and Bounds   A land description in which boundaries are described by courses, directions, distances, and monuments.

Mortgage   A lien or claim against real property given by the buyer to the lender as security for money borrowed. Under government-insured or loan-guarantee provisions, the payments may include escrow amounts covering taxes, hazard insurance, water charges, and special assessments. Mortgages generally run from 10 to 30 years, during which the loan is to be paid off.

Mortgage Commitment   A written notice from the bank or other lending institution saying it will advance mortgage funds in a specified amount to enable a buyer to purchase a house.

Mortgage Insurance   Insurance written by an independent mortgage insurance company protecting the mortgage lender against loss incurred by a mortgage default, thus enabling the lender to lend a higher percentage of the sale price.

Mortgage Insurance Premium   The payment made by a borrower to the lender for transmittal to HUD to help defray the cost of the FHA mortgage insurance program and to provide a reserve fund to protect lenders against loss in insured mortgage transactions. In FHA insured mortgages this represents an annual rate of one-half of 1 percent paid by the mortgagor on a monthly basis.

Mortgage Note   A written agreement to repay a loan. The agreement is secured by a mortgage, serves as proof of an indebtedness, and states the manner in which it shall be paid. The note states the actual amount of the debt that the mortgage secures and renders the mortgagor personally responsible for repayment.

Mortgage (Open-End)   A mortgage with a provision that permits borrowing additional money in the future without refinancing the loan or paying additional financing charges. Open-end provisions often limit such borrowing to no more than would raise the balance to the original loan figure.

Mortgagee   The holder of a mortgage. The party to whom a mortgage is made, generally the lender.

Mortgagee Policy   Also called a "Loan Policy." A title insurance policy insuring a mortgagee, or beneficiary under a deed of trust, against loss caused by invalidity or unenforceability of a lien, or loss of priority of the mortgage or deed of trust.

Mortgagor   A person who mortgages property. A person who executes a mortgage, generally the property owner.

Multiple Listing Service (MLS)   The pooling in a central bureau of listings of properties for sale. These listings are held individually by members of a group of real estate brokers, with the agreement that any member of the group may sell the properties and, in the case of a sale, the commission will be divided between the broker making the sale and the broker who filed the listing.

Muniments of Title   Written evidence (documents) that an owner possesses to prove his or her title to property.

N

Note   Also called "Promissory Note." A written promise to pay a sum of money, usually at a specified interest rate, at a stated time to a named payee.

O

Owner's Policy A policy of title insurance insuring an owner of real estate against loss occasioned by defects in, liens against, or unmarketability of the owner's title.

P

Plat Also called a "Plat Map." A map dividing a parcel of land into lots, as in a subdivision. A plat book contains the plat maps for a given area.

Points Sometimes called "Discount Points." A point is 1 percent of the amount of the mortgage loan. For example, if a loan is for $25,000, one point is $250. Points are charged by a lender to raise the yield on his or her loan at a time when money is tight, interest rates are high, and there is a legal limit to the interest rate that can be charged on a mortgage. Buyers are prohibited from paying points on HUD or Veterans Administration guaranteed loans (sellers can pay, however). On a conventional mortgage, points may be paid by either buyer or seller or split between them.

Premium The amount payable for an insurance policy.

Prepayment Payment of mortgage loan, or part of it, before its due date. Mortgage agreements often restrict the right of prepayment either by limiting the amount that can be prepaid in any one year or charging a penalty for prepayment. The Federal Housing Administration does not permit such restrictions in FHA insured mortgages.

Prescriptive Easement A right to use another's property that is not inconsistent with the owner's rights and that is acquired by an open, notorious, adverse, and continuous use for the statutory period, for example, 20 years.

Principal (1) A sum of money owed as a debt on which interest is payable. (2) A person who empowers another to act as his or her representative or agent. (3) The person having prime responsibility for an obligation as distinguished from one who acts as a surety or endorser.

Purchase Money Mortgage A mortgage given by a purchaser to a seller on the subject property to secure payment of a part of the purchase price.

Q

Quitclaim Deed   A deed that transfers whatever interest a maker of the deed may have in a particular parcel of land. A quitclaim deed is often given to clear the title when the grantor's interest in a property is questionable. By accepting such a deed the buyer assumes all the risks. Such a deed makes no warranties as to the title, but simply transfers to the buyer whatever interest the grantor has. (See also Deed.)

R

Real Estate   Also called "Real Property." (1) Land and anything permanently affixed to the land, such as buildings, fences, and those things attached to the buildings, such as light fixtures, plumbing and heating fixtures, or other such items that would be personal property if not attached. (2) May refer to rights in real property as well as the property itself.

Real Estate Broker   A middleman or agent who buys and sells real estate for a company, firm, or individual on a commission basis. The broker does not have title to the property, but generally represents the owner.

Recording   The noting in a public office of the details of a legal document—such as a deed or mortgage—affecting the title to real estate. When such an instrument is properly recorded, it is considered to be a matter of public record. Legally, that means that all subsequent purchasers are deemed to have constrictive knowledge of that information.

Refinancing   The process of the same mortgagor paying off one loan with the proceeds from another loan.

Reinsurance   The noting in a public office of the details of a legal document—such as a deed or mortgage—affecting the title to real estate. When such an instrument is properly recorded, it is considered to be a matter of public record. Legally, that means that all subsequent purchasers are deemed to have constrictive knowledge of that information.

Release   The noting in a public office of the details of a legal document—such as a deed or mortgage—affecting the title to real estate. When such an instrument is properly recorded, it is considered to be a matter of public record. Legally, that means that all subsequent purchasers are deemed to have constrictive knowledge of that information.

Restrictions   The noting in a public office of the details of a legal document—such as a deed or mortgage—affecting the title to real estate. When such an instrument is properly recorded, it is considered to be a matter of public record. Legally, that means that all subsequent purchasers are deemed to have constrictive knowledge of that information.

Restrictive Covenants   Restrictive covenants are private restrictions limiting the use of real property. They are created by deed and may "run with the land," binding all subsequent purchasers of the land, or may be "personal" and binding only between the original seller and buyer. The determination whether a covenant runs with the land or is personal is governed by the language of the covenant, the intent of the parties, and the law in the state where the land is situated. Restrictive covenants that run with the land are encumbrances and may affect the value and marketability of title. Restrictive covenants may limit the density of buildings per acre, regulate size, style, or price range of buildings to be erected, or prevent particular businesses from operating or minority groups from owning or occupying homes in a given area. (This latter discriminatory covenant is unconstitutional and has been declared unenforceable by the U.S. Supreme Court.)

Riparian Rights   The rights of owners of lands bordering watercourses which relate to the water and its use.

S

Sales Agreement   A contract entered into between a buyer and seller, setting forth the terms, provisions, and conditions of a sale of real estate.

Sale and Leaseback   The sale of an asset to a buyer who immediately leases it back to the seller.

Search   A careful exploration and perusal of the public records in an effort to find all recorded instruments relating to a particular chain of title.

Second Mortgage   A mortgage ranking in priority immediately below a first mortgage.

Special Assessments   A special tax imposed on property, individual lots, or all property in the immediate area for road construction, sidewalks, sewers, street lights, etc.

Special Lien   A lien that binds a specified piece of property, unlike a general lien, which is levied against all one's assets. It creates a right to retain something of value belonging to another person as compensation for labor, material, or money expended in that person's behalf. In some localities it is called "particular" lien or "specific" lien. (See Lien.)

Special Warranty Deed   A deed in which the grantor conveys title to the grantee and agrees to protect the grantee against title defects or claims asserted by the grantor and those persons whose right to assert a claim against the title arose during the period the grantor held title to the property. In a special warranty deed the grantor guarantees to the grantee that he or she has done nothing during the time he or she held title to the property which has, or which might in the future, impair the grantee's title.

State Stamps   A state tax, in the forms of stamps, required on deeds and mortgages when real estate title passes from one owner to another. The amount of stamps required varies with each state.

Subordination   The act or process by which a person's rights are ranked below the rights of others. For example, a second mortgagee's rights are subordinate to those of the first mortgagee.

Surety   (1) A person who agrees to be responsible for a debt or obligation of another. (2) The pledge or agreement by which one undertakes responsibility for the debt or obligation of another.

Survey   A map or plat made by a licensed surveyor showing the results of measuring the land with its elevations, improvements, boundaries, and its relationship to surrounding tracts of land. A survey is often required by the lender to assure him or her that a building is actually sited on the land according to its legal description.

T

Tax   As applied to real estate, an enforced charge imposed on persons, property or income, to be used to support the state. The governing body in turn utilizes the funds in the best interest of the general public.

Title   (1) A combination of all the elements that constitute the highest legal right to own, possess, use, control, enjoy, and dispose of real estate or an inheritable right or interest therein. (2) The rights of ownership recognized and protected by law.

Title Covenants   Covenants ordinarily inserted in conveyance and in transfers of title to real estate for the purpose of giving protection to the purchaser against possible insufficiency of the title received. A group of such covenants known as "Common Law Covenants" includes: covenants against encumbrances; covenants for further assurance (in other words, to do whatever is necessary to rectify title deficiencies); covenants of good right and authority to convey; covenants of quiet enjoyment; covenants of seisin; covenants of warranty. (See also Covenant or Warranty.)

Title Defect   (1) Any possible or patent claim or right outstanding in a chain of title that is adverse to the claim of ownership. (2) Any material irregularity in the execution or effect of an instrument in the chain of title.

Title Insurance Policy   A contract of title insurance under which the insurer, in keeping with the terms of the policy, agrees to indemnify the insured against loss arising from claims against the insured interest.

Title Plant   Also called "Abstract Plant" in some areas. A geographically filed assemblage of title information that helps in expediting title examinations, such as copies of previous attorneys' opinions, abstracts, tax searches, and copies of take-offs of the public records.

Title Search or Examination   A check of the title records, generally at the local courthouse, to make sure the buyer is purchasing a house from the legal owner and there are no liens, overdue special assessments, or other claims or outstanding restrictive covenants filed in the record, which would adversely affect the marketability or value of title.

Trustee   A party who is given legal responsibility to hold property in the best interest of or "for the benefit of" another. The trustee is one placed in a position of responsibility for another, a responsibility enforceable in a court of law. (See also Deed of Trust.)

U

Underwriter   An insurance company that issues insurance policies to the public or to another insurer.

V

Variable Interest Rate   Also called "Flexible Interest Rate." An interest rate that fluctuates as the prevailing rate moves up or down. In mortgages, there are usually maximums as to the frequency and amount of fluctuation.

Veterans Administration (VA) Loans   Housing loans to veterans by banks, savings and loans, or other lenders that are guaranteed by the Veterans Administration, thus enabling veterans to buy a residence with little or no down payment.

W

Waiver   The voluntary and intentional relinquishment of a known right, claim, or privilege.

Warranty   In a broad sense, an agreement or undertaking by a seller to be responsible for present or future losses of the purchaser occasioned by deficiency or defect in the quality, condition, or quantity of the thing sold. In a stricter sense, the provision or provisions in a deed, lease, or other instrument conveying or transferring an estate or interest in real estate under which the seller becomes liable to the purchaser for defects in or encumbrances on the title. (See also Title Covenants.)

Will   A testamentary disposition of property, usually in a form prescribed by law, that takes effect upon death.

X

Y

Z

Zoning   Laws passed by local governments regulating the size, type, structure, nature, and use of land or buildings.

Zoning Ordinances   The acts of an authorized local government establishing building codes and setting forth regulations for property land usage.

Index

Index

Index

Index

Index

About the Author

Daniel J. Nahorney is a real estate expert and is the coauthor of *How to Increase the Value of Your Home.* He is also a journalist, business writer, and magazine editor.